WHEN A

Soulmate

SAYS **NO**

WHEN A *Soulmate* SAYS NO

A MEMOIR
AMANDA TRENFIELD

PEPPER PRESS

First published in 2022 by Pepper Press, an imprint of Fair Play Publishing
PO Box 4101, Balgowlah Heights, NSW 2093, Australia

www.fairplaypublishing.com.au
sales@fairplaypublishing.com.au

ISBN: 978-1-925914-43-6
ISBN: 978-1-925914-44-3 (ePub)

This book is a memoir. It reflects the author's present recollections
of experiences over time, and depicts actual events in her life.
The names of some individuals and places, or identifying characteristics
of individuals or places may have been changed to respect their privacy.
In all instances where real names or places have been used,
the author has sought the prior permission of the individual.

If any reader is affected by any of the issues raised in this book,
please contact an organisation such as Lifeline (www.lifeline.org.au)
or Beyond Blue (www.beyondblue.org.au) for advice and support.

Cover design by Lisa Rafferty
Typesetting by Leslie Priestley
Photo of Amanda Trenfield by Andrea Francolini
Printed by SOS Media, Sydney

All inquiries should be made to the Publisher via sales@fairplaypublishing.com.au

NATIONAL
LIBRARY
OF AUSTRALIA

A catalogue record of this book is available from the National Library of Australia.

A Soulmate is the one person
whose love is powerful enough
to motivate you to meet your soul,
to do the emotional work of self-discovery,
of awakening

KENNY LOGGINS

The depth of emotional authenticity and raw vulnerability expressed in When a Soulmate Says No is increasingly rare. Beginning with the total annihilation of her heart, Amanda's story transitions beautifully into one of bravery, honesty, and deep transformation. The quest to align with her soul, and journey back to who she was all along, is a compelling read that had me holding my breath and cheering her on from the very first chapter. If you have experienced heartache and loss, allow yourself to be guided by Amanda, and enjoy the feeling of living this nearly unbelievable story by her side. Brava!

NANCY LEVIN
Best-selling author of *Setting Boundaries Will Set You Free*
and Founder of Levin Life Coach Academy

How do you know when you've met your soulmate? Amanda knew it instantly in every fiber of her being. What came next was a surprising exploration driven by universal intervention to a place deep within. A place leading back to her authentic self and the discovery of her soul power.

LAURA E SUMMERS
Co-Author of #1 International Best-Seller *Women Who Rise*

When A Soulmate Says No is a love story of a different kind - a raw, intimate, and provocative journey back to self. Amanda teaches us that out of pain can come substantial growth; that getting shaken to the core is not an inglorious end, but instead opens us to the dynamic possibility of a glorious new beginning - the rebuilding of life that renders us our own hero. I was riveted from the first pages and deeply enlightened the rest of the way.

NANCY PICKARD
#1 International Best-selling Author of *Bigger Better Braver*

Contents

1.
You Took
My Breath Away

I wasn't expecting a formal dinner with cheerful conference attendees in the beautiful Margaret River to turn my life upside down. I had a good life. I wasn't looking to upend it—or was I?

I had decided only the week earlier to attend the three-day event with my husband. It wasn't in the family holiday plan and we had to arrange care for the children, but I saw it as a perfect opportunity for us to reconnect as we had become quite distant. I believed that time away from the stress of everyday life was the perfect remedy to reignite our relationship.

I had also been working very hard, so exploring boutique wineries with their cosy cellar doors, sampling Rosé, Semillon and Shiraz was just too tempting to pass up. Enjoying expertly crafted wines with the opportunity to decompress and relax in a country setting is one of my favourite pastimes.

We entered the magnificent oak-panelled dining room, taking our seats at a long, elegantly laid table. My husband sat to my left, and quickly engaged in conversation with another couple.

As I settled into my seat, I looked up, and immediately lost my breath. When our eyes met there was an instant familiarity that ran deeper than water-cooler chat. Those eyes had locked before. Twelve years earlier. His name was Jason. I hadn't forgotten.

Throughout the dinner, I was my usual animated and conversational self. I was, after all, in sales. The group chatted happily, all of us enjoying an excellent degustation of Western Australian delicacies cooked with attention and pride.

As entree was served Jason offered me a sip of his wine—to taste the robust Margaret River old-vine Shiraz. After a little banter and coaxing, I accepted.

Our repartee was enchanting to me. Our tête-à-têtes and pleasure of each other's company was exceedingly apparent from the very first moment. We had such a natural, easy connection; I soon recognised the evening was going to afford more than delicious food and wine. I smiled.

Over the course of the evening my attraction to Jason developed. I soon became aware of his every breath and I unconsciously mirrored his pace. I caught myself, embarrassingly, looking at his chest through his slim-fitted white evening shirt. Yes, he had a fit, toned and attractive body, but was it his chest I was drawn to?

When dessert was served, he offered me a sample of his decadent and oozy chocolate pudding. I declined, but he scooped up a generous spoonful and fed me across the table anyway. He displayed a level of familiarity normally reserved for close friends or lovers. If anyone had been watching us, they would have been at least curious as to the nature of our relationship. My husband didn't notice the pudding exchange, or any of my other interactions with Jason over the course of the dinner.

By the time the group left the restaurant late in the evening, all my senses were on high alert. It was abundantly clear to me the energy between Jason and me was somehow charged. I instinctively understood though this was more than just lust. I also understood it was more than simply physical attraction, but I just couldn't put my finger on it.

At the hotel bar, Jason bought me a glass of my favourite Rosé. We looked into each other's eyes—his dark and mysterious, mine big and brown—and clinked glasses. The electricity between us was strong, raw and unfathomably intense. It travelled to my core. It was so intense, I needed to break eye contact. He. We. The energy. It was electric. My body was completely charged. I was completely 'on'.

I loved talking with him. I felt warm, relaxed and safe in his presence. I felt I could truly be myself—on a level I wasn't familiar with. It was a feeling I realised I hadn't enjoyed in a long, long time—perhaps even ever. Sure, we would laugh, joke and banter as if old friends but the deepening connection through our eyes was undeniable.

In one conversation my husband, Jason and I were talking about overseas adventures we all enjoyed in our university days. Midway through the storytelling I unintentionally and unconsciously gravitated to Jason's side and faced my husband. When I noticed what I had done, I tried to subtly reorient myself to put equal distance between the three of us—to ensure it wasn't that obvious. It was though: I knew. Jason knew. We both knew it was more than harmless flirting. It was real.

There was a time late in the evening when we were in our intense, delicious bubble of conversation where I unintentionally brought my right thumb to my heart space and rubbed it. He saw that. He saw *me* in that moment. We saw each other. I had to concentrate on breathing.

My behaviour that evening was uncharacteristic. I stayed out way longer than I normally would. I'm usually an early-to-bed-early-to-rise type. But this was no ordinary evening. I was in no hurry to leave the energy, in no hurry to leave our connection. In fact, I wanted time to stand still. I wanted to remain in the energy, our energy, forever.

The bar called last drinks, and the evening (now the early morning) came to an end. The goodbye was overt, open and revealing of our connection. We enjoyed a body-hugging embrace where I whispered into his ear, "This isn't over, I need to see you again." He put his hands tightly on my waist and pulled me close. "Yes," he replied. It was all I needed to hear.

As I danced back to my room feeling completely vulnerable, but also unexpectedly whole, I couldn't wipe the smile from my face.

I had never felt anything like this before. I had never experienced this sensation. I didn't understand the energy. It was an out-of-body, or perhaps an 'in-body' experience.

I now know without hesitation, without question, without any doubt in my mind, my body or my heart that the energy we experienced that evening was our souls connecting.

I scarcely slept. I lay in bed, questioning if the night I had just experienced had actually happened. Was it even real? Or had I just enjoyed a seductive, out-of-this world, vivid dream? I lay silently in the darkened room, next to my husband, until the sun rose. As I lay in quiet contemplation though, I knew it was real.

I wasn't going to attend breakfast but soon realised that if Jason was on the first bus to the airport, it would be my only chance to see him again. So, I showered, changed and met my husband in the restaurant. I could see Jason a few tables away.

My husband left for the conference, leaving me alone to enjoy my coffee and croissant. At that moment, Jason looked up and saw me. I lost my breath as our eyes connected.

He approached and without speaking, just sat down—the most natural thing in the world to do. He confirmed he was off to the airport before lunch. He asked what I was doing for the morning, to which I replied, "Nothing in particular." He then volunteered that he would skip the morning conference session. We said our somewhat self-conscious goodbyes and he left the breakfast.

It Couldn't End There

When I retreated to my hotel room, I immediately knew I needed to see him again. That awkward goodbye in the restaurant could not be the final time we spoke. I paced around my room, summoning the courage to call him. Within minutes, I had found the courage, or it found me.

I dialled his room and asked if he wanted to go for a walk together. He enthusiastically agreed and was at my door within five minutes. He turned up in a tee-shirt and jeans (it was 15 degrees). I reiterated we were going for a walk, and we left.

Once he had agreed to meet, I have a clear recollection of going straight to the mirror to check how awful I looked after too much wine and barely any sleep. As I looked in the mirror though, I instinctively knew it didn't actually matter what I looked like. My looks were not the attraction. I knew at that moment the way I looked that morning didn't matter at all.

It didn't matter that I had my tight black jeans on with my new floral top under a bright-purple puffer jacket, or that my dark hair was a curly mess. And it didn't matter that I was carrying a few too many kilos or that my makeup, no matter how hard I tried, couldn't conceal the dark circles under my eyes. I knew in an instant he wouldn't notice what I was wearing or the style of my hair, just like I didn't notice the colour of his jeans or tee-shirt. It was in that instant I was reminded that this was much deeper.

It was a beautiful clear and crisp morning. The sun was shining, and the birds were chirping. We wandered through the gorgeous Western Australian bushland of native olive trees and long grasses by a stream of trickling water. It felt like I was the lead character in a romantic Hollywood movie, walking through the luscious natural environment with a gorgeous man by my side—just the music was missing!

The conversation was tough for us both, but clearly required. I opened with something like, "I felt nervous with you last night. It was very intense, but I need you to know."

A few steps along the bush track he replied, "You're not alone with those feelings, I felt the same way."

My heart was in my throat, my body on edge, and all I could think in that moment was I didn't want to be anywhere else in the world.

I only wanted to be there, in the beautiful landscape, with him by my side.

We found somewhere to sit, side by side, on my jacket. Our connection by now was undeniable. The energy between us was beyond anything I had ever experienced. Neither of us really knew what to say, or what to do. We shared very little eye contact. He was clearly taken aback at our connection as well.

He mentioned we could have been seated at any one of the tables last night and yet we sat where we did. He recognised we were meant to connect. Our meeting was always destined to be more than a passing "Hi."

Words failed me. All I could do was nod in agreement.

His first question to me was, "Are you happy?"

I was stunned. I was speechless. I couldn't answer him. I just sat there looking at him. I hadn't really thought about it.

Life was just too busy to ask myself the question. While I tried to find the words—any words—to answer, he declared that he didn't want to break up a marriage; he had witnessed too many ugly, destructive divorces, and he didn't want that for me. He had clearly thought this through. I sensed he hadn't managed to get much sleep either.

The next instant I felt a sudden tension from him. "We shouldn't let this go any further. We shouldn't have any contact moving forward. We shouldn't see each other again."

I was momentarily speechless, but I certainly wasn't ready to let him go. After a minute or two of silence, he relaxed once again, settled into the space ever so close to me, and took my hand in his. We sat together, shoulder by shoulder, enjoying the feeling of pure contentment, pure bliss—dare I say, pure happiness—whilst listening to the trickling stream below.

I broke the silence by saying, "I think you should kiss me." He looked directly into my eyes and countered, "Just kiss you?" My heart skipped another beat. "Yes, it's all I'm capable of right now."

Our lips touched and I was home. Really home for the first time in my life. We eventually broke for air and he looked deeply into my eyes. "Oh no," he whispered as we drank each other in.

For the next half hour or so we sat, talked and kissed in this tranquil, romantic spot. Our kisses were loving, long, calm, familiar, intense, passionate, and yet restricted. We held hands, touched legs. I rested my head on his shoulder whilst overlooking the creek. He reciprocated, resting his head on mine. I wanted time to freeze, and I said so. I just couldn't let him go.

He reiterated that we shouldn't stay in contact, although visibly struggling as our kissing intensified. Our passion and desire for each other was abundantly clear. There was now no hiding from our feelings, no hiding from our chemistry, no hiding from our connection. Our armours were dropped, our weaponry put away.

He broke the silence by saying, "This will consume us. This will consume us."

It was all I wanted though—to be consumed by him. To not move. To stay in the feelings of pure bliss, pure joy and pure contentment for the rest of my life.

With nothing more to say, with my mind bewildered, my body awake, my emotional energy spent and my heart now full of love, we left our spot amongst the olive trees.

We walked slowly along the bush track, holding hands and drawing each other close until the resort came into view. We didn't speak. We just enjoyed the experience of being together, in perplexed but wondrous bliss. We dropped hands as we neared the resort, kissed and whispered a short goodbye. I couldn't prolong our farewell; I was in too much distress. I realised I never wanted to utter that word to him for the rest of my life.

Oh. My. God.

I left Margaret River a different woman.

I knew in my heart, in my soul, in the very fabric of my being that

I had profoundly changed. I couldn't articulate the feelings, the sensations, the in-body experience. The connectedness I experienced with Jason was at a level impossible to describe. All I knew for certain was this one encounter, in the most unlikely of places, under the most unusual of circumstances, had dramatically altered my life.

The next few days were a complete blur. I couldn't make any sense of my feelings. I couldn't escape the unrelenting thoughts of Jason. I certainly couldn't fathom how I could possibly resume my normal life—a full-time financial services career, the care of two young children, household chores, social engagements, being a wife. All I did understand was the successful, comfortable and somewhat predictable life I had spent 20 years building was of no consequence. I simply didn't care.

I had just met my soulmate. What could possibly be more important than that?

Welcome to my awakening ...

Moving Forward

My anxiety was dangerously elevated, and I was having a terrible time sleeping. I didn't understand what was happening to me. For the first time, I was questioning how I was living my life, questioning what my carefully planned future looked like, even questioning who I was!

I experienced a violent physical event on the bus heading in to work a week later. I became irrationally irritated as the driver continued to let people board even though there were already a dozen of us standing. As the bus approached the Sydney Harbour Bridge, I started feeling ill. My stomach was full, knotted and queasy. I became so dizzy I thought I would faint. I broke out in a full body sweat. Within minutes my white business blouse was soaked through. I then realised with alarm I needed a bathroom, and quickly. By the grace of God, I made it to the city.

I managed, finally, to compose myself enough to rejoin the people on the streets of Sydney, but made it only as far as the closest cafe. I slumped into a chair and ordered a peppermint tea. The physical sensations had subsided, but I was utterly exhausted. My energy was depleted and it wasn't even 8.00 a.m. The city was too frantic, too noisy, too soul-destroying. I took the bus straight home and went to bed. My world had been shaken to its core—my emotional-physical-spiritual core.

Lying in bed, I endeavoured to separate my encounter with Jason in Margaret River from him as a person—who I really didn't know. I tried to reconcile how I was living my life and the reality of my present circumstances. I also tried to understand what the sensations in my body were trying to tell me. What the hell was going on?

I reflected on how the evening with Jason unfolded. My only expectation had been to enjoy some great food, wine and conversation amidst the vineyards. By the end of the night my soul—not just my heart—was completely engulfed, completely satisfied.

I reminisced on the way we connected. How we were drawn to each other, how we both recognised our unique connection. How the depth of our stares into each other's eyes reunited our souls. I knew it at that moment. It was an 'ah-ha' moment that quickly became a profound revelation, and it took my breath away. We had shared a past life together and our souls wanted more.

The thought the night would end was only buoyed by the certain knowledge it wasn't over. We were not over. We couldn't possibly be over. This was purely the initial soul recognition. Then would come the recalibration—the reorganisation of my life and his life. The two of us would then come together. Of course we would. I did not—and could not—entertain any other outcome, any other future.

Then the heartbreaking realisation hit me in my core. It was lightning fast, and it was horrifying. Devastating. It was (almost) unimaginable. But in that instant, I *knew* it to be true.

My marriage was over. I sat in the energy, in the profound

revelation, for hours. I didn't move. I couldn't. I just lay on my bed, and I cried.

❖

The next chapter of my life had already begun. I had no idea how the next few days, weeks and months would unfold but I intuitively understood I needed to keep the focus on love. I needed to be brave enough to not only acknowledge the end of my marriage, but to find a way to move through this next chapter with compassion, positivity and strength.

It was at that moment I made a deliberate decision to consciously shift my perspective from sadness to gratitude. I was not to be sad my marriage was ending, but to be thankful and grateful for our time and experiences together; for the life we had enjoyed as a couple for many years; for our delightful, healthy and happy children.

My husband would always be incredibly important to me, and his health and well-being became my foremost concern. I had to be considerate, I had to be thoughtful, I had to be respectful. But I also had to be authentic to my truth.

To have experienced what I did with Jason and then pretend it didn't happen and go on to play 'happy family' would be inauthentic, and damn disrespectful to the union I had enjoyed with my husband. If my future no longer included the man I married, how dare I continue in a marriage that could no longer be sustained in honesty and truth? How dare I dishonour him and our amazing years together? How dare I rob him of his future happiness by staying when I knew in my soul I was no longer home?

Less than a month after meeting Jason, having had no communication with him since our time at Margaret River, I ended my 14-year relationship with my husband.

The woman who had always been so careful, so planned, so organised and clear about the path her life would take had just made the most dramatic decision of her life, affecting those dearest to her— her family.

The Journey Back to Me

The months that followed were the most emotionally, mentally, physically and spiritually traumatic of my life. All I wanted to do was retreat into my inner world and begin the process of healing. I dreamt of escaping to a luxurious resort in the country, cocooning under a doona, and ordering delicious hot chocolates and carrot cake to my door. It was what I desperately craved, but the reality of my life all too quickly brought me crashing back to earth. It was simply not an option.

I wasn't born into money; I have worked full time my whole adult life. Although I had created a life of comfort for my family and myself, I wasn't in a position to resign from my job to focus full time on myself. The machinations of daily life didn't respect my acute desire to switch the world off and retreat inward.

I thought about all the people who were depending on me: my children, my husband, my ageing parents, my team at work and my clients. The food still needed to be prepared, the washing still needed to be done, the mortgage still needed to be paid and the daycare fees were steep.

I struggled every morning just getting out of bed. Joining the city workers squashed like sardines on the bus, then fighting my way to the office through the noise and construction that was the downtown business district of Sydney. It was utterly soul-destroying. As if my soul wasn't going through enough!

Turning up to the office every day displaying my professional game face for my colleagues and clients required every ounce of fortitude I could muster. It was abject torture.

Pretending to family and friends I was in control and managing the excruciatingly painful life changes I inflicted on my family required daily Oscar-winning performances.

Raising two gorgeous daughters, one just out of nappies, knowing full well I had just robbed them of an upbringing in a stable family unit broke my heart every day.

But through the devastation, heartache and dramatic upheaval that was my life, I was simultaneously preparing myself for my new beginning with Jason. I was sustained by my unqualified belief we would find our way back to each other. Of course we would. We had to. It was the only way I could see my future. It was the only way I could see my happiness.

He was my soulmate.

I had found him. He had found me. We had found each other.

Let the Healing Begin

I am here, as I am arriving ...

I took another day off work. The idea of traipsing into the city was just too much to contemplate. I said goodbye to my husband, dropped the children at daycare, and retreated to the silence of my bedroom. I closed the curtains and jumped back into bed. I lay in the stillness and silence for hours.

My life had been turned upside down and I'd been spun around so fast, that as hard as I tried, I just couldn't find my balance. I willed my brain to offer any sliver, any morsel of advice that would help me find a way through. Anything that would help me make sense of my situation. It wouldn't. I was completely and utterly lost. There were so, so many tears. I fell asleep.

I woke up sometime mid-afternoon with a start. The cogs had started turning in my brain during my sleep, my unconsciousness delivering the advice I had asked for earlier that day. It was short, clear and direct. I didn't need to have it all figured out immediately, I just needed to begin ... somewhere. I needed to move forward by taking just one step at a time. What I needed to do, to let my healing begin, was go back to basics.

This story, dear reader, is my mud map of how I survived the experience of meeting my soulmate and not enjoying my happily ever after—at least, not in the way I had so audaciously dreamed.

My sincere wish in sharing this personal account of heartbreak and loss is to demonstrate the incredible power of hope. Although it may seem like the end of the world, an experience like this can be the spark, the catalyst, that leads to a courageous, transformative and authentic life.

The journey isn't easy, but I invite you to come take it with me anyway.

2.
Back to Basics

Journalling

As I returned to the hotel room after my walk with Jason I breathed a sigh of relief. My husband was still at the conference. I had the room to myself. There were so many thoughts racing through my mind I simply couldn't make sense of anything. How am I feeling? Where am I aching? Am I going mad? Did I really just have that experience or is it part of an elaborate plot to bring me down? Has sanity left my body? Will I survive this?

I grabbed the only pieces of paper I could find—my printed travel itinerary—and began frantically writing on the back. I had only two sheets of paper, so I wrote in a very, very small cursive hand. I had to make sure no detail of our time together would ever be forgotten. Although I couldn't even begin to comprehend how in that moment, I knew this experience would change the course of my life. I wrote at the desk, without a pause, for an hour.

The outpouring of emotion through the words on the pages was cathartic. It was a source of self-expression that allowed me to go deeper and process what I had just experienced.

I didn't have the right words, but I did the best I could to describe my physical, emotional and spiritual reactions to Jason. It helped soothe my soul just a little. When I finished my written recollections, I put the pieces of paper in my handbag—hiding them in the secret side pocket on the off-chance my husband needed something from my bag over the next few days.

I hadn't kept a diary since I was an angst-ridden teenager, growing up on the beach in Australia. I somehow knew though it would be an invaluable resource for my life going forward. So, when I returned to Sydney, buying a new diary was one of the first things I did. When I came home from my shopping excursion I made a coffee, sat down on my sofa, and wrote the first entry in my new purple-and-floral-fabric-covered diary.

> *It all happened so fast. A matter of hours that started as a friendly dinner, to where the centre of my soul—not just my heart—was completely consumed. The way we connected was complete. The way my breathing changed; the way I was physically drawn to his side. The way our eyes connected our old souls. We have been together in a past life and my soul wanted more.*
>
> *Reflecting now, a few days later, I am in a world of struggle. I ache in my soul for him. I consider the possibilities of a life together. How it would work practically and logistically. It's like his soul has been placed right in front of me at the right time. To begin a new story. To begin a new chapter with my soulmate.*
>
> *I sit here now, full of emotion, crying to 'Nothing's Going to Stop Us Now'—a hit by Starship in the 1980s, and thinking of when I am going to reunite with him. He consumes my every thought. He consumes me.*

With tears still streaming down my face, I closed my diary and tucked it away safely in my bedside drawer. I felt physically and emotionally drained, but also strangely comforted by the words expressed on the pages.

It increased my determination to find a way forward, to draw on all my strength and courage, and ensure everyone was cared for emotionally and financially. I was resolute—I would do whatever it took to minimise the stress and anxiety on my family and friends—

the people who meant the world to me. I was, of course, also emphatic that my future was with Jason and that we would be living in soulmate bliss within weeks.

Little did I know, writing that first diary entry, I had such a long, long, long way to go. Had my future path been fully illuminated—if I had any inkling of the challenges, despair and heartache that awaited me—I may never have embarked on the journey. I might have decided I didn't have the energy to even begin the fight back to me. In truth, the Amanda of now knows in her heart and soul, had my entire journey been revealed to me at the time, you would not be reading this book.

A few days later, my mood had completely transformed and my imagination was once again in full swing, envisioning my future with Jason in spectacular colour and detail. We were clearly going to end up together—how could there be any other outcome? I was 'jumping for joy' enthusiastic for my imminent new beginning.

My journal began to serve another important function—it became my to-do list. I planned the sale of my assets, workshopped how I could perform my job from another state for the inevitable move to join Jason, and began a list of the pros and cons of houses near him. With my children and his, there would absolutely be the need for a bigger house! I was preparing to begin my new life with my soulmate.

A few weeks later, though, the confidence in my certain future had been crushed and my spirit was in critical condition. There had still been no contact from Jason. The waves of emotions I was experiencing, not just day to day, but sometimes hour to hour, was akin to a tsunami. I have a vivid recollection of sitting at a work conference, keeping up appearances and (not) listening to some macroeconomic update, but instead focusing my attention on writing a letter to Jason in my journal:

I don't understand how, given how amazing and rare it is to find a soulmate in this life, we are not together and living in absolute bliss. I struggle in my darker days to want to exist in this world if you are not with me.

I truly question, having had you so briefly in my life, and with the knowledge of how rare this is—why bother?

I was on the verge of tears when a terrifying prospect hit me—was it possible that he did not feel the same way? I urgently needed to escape—this conference was certainly no place for a hysterical woman—so I packed up my belongings and with my head down, weaved my way through the hundreds of clients that were (hopefully) not paying me any attention.

I walked across the road to the park and slumped down onto a bench seat. I was not aware who was around me, or even if I was crying. I was numb and in acute pain at the same time. It felt like I was in an alternate universe, somehow not even on the earth. It didn't make any sense, but so much of my experience didn't make any sense to me at that point. I eventually peeled myself off the park bench, hailed a taxi and went home to bed. Again.

Even now it's easy to recall the tumultuous ache of those early days. When the recollections swell in my chest, I try to take a moment to centre myself and give grace to that version of Amanda. I owe her so much and I'm so proud of her! After all, she's the Amanda who kept going, the Amanda who persevered on the journey back to herself.

I managed to write most days, usually as I jumped into bed knowing I wouldn't be disturbed. I would write whatever felt right, whatever I needed to get out of my head. Some days I would spend five minutes writing away quite disconnected, other times I would write furiously for an hour. Often, it would be a mess of random thoughts and feelings. Most times, there were tears.

It helped me though. It allowed me to feel my emotions in a visceral way and integrate a deeper level of understanding of my situation. It helped me process my thoughts and prioritise my next steps. It also opened the possibility of viewing my experience from different perspectives. Sometimes this elevated my soul; other times it almost destroyed it.

I also reread my diary entries which served a beneficial purpose— it highlighted just how far I had come on my journey. This gave me the strength and fortitude to take just one more forward step. It also allowed me to talk myself back off the ledge when I feared I couldn't continue. Journalling gave me the courage I needed, that I so desperately craved in those dark, early days, and I am so grateful to have re-engaged with the practice.

Yoga

I had been a member of the in-house gym in my city office building for a few years but generally participated in the aerobic classes or challenged myself on the treadmill. Not long after meeting Jason, however, it became clear the high-intensity exercise was too strenuous for my already over-taxed system. The fact that I wasn't sleeping well certainly didn't help. I needed a different form of physical exercise; one that didn't punish my body and drain the infinitesimal amount of energy I had available. I consulted the schedule and signed up for a yoga class.

I had experimented with various forms of yoga over the years, but was by no means a regular class attender or a convert to the practice. At this time, in the midst of such pain and anxiety, I decided to reconnect with the practice. It not only promised to relieve the anguish I was feeling but it also provided an essential escape from my demanding job in the middle of a hectic workday. It afforded me the opportunity to let go of my corporate face, if just for an hour.

I remember that first class so clearly. The room was warm and dark, lit only by a large salt lamp in the back corner emitting an orange glow. I arrived early, walking in with my head down, no smile on my face and no spring in my step. I laid out my mat at the very back of the room.

As I lay there, waiting patiently for the instructor to begin the class, I began to cry. Not a big wail or even a sniffle. I just closed my eyes and tears began to roll down my cheeks. I tried desperately not to draw any attention to myself. I would not have coped if anyone had asked me if I was okay. I clearly wasn't. Thankfully, I was spared an inquisition.

I don't remember any of the specifics, I just did my best to move with the rest of the yogis—to try and fit in, to belong. The class provided me with the opportunity to just be with myself, and I needed the peace and solitude in every fibre of my being. It also took me out of my head—from my never-ending thoughts of Jason—and delivered me into my body. That respite alone was worth its weight in gold. When the class ended I slunk out, showered, put my work armour back on, and finished my work day.

I was hopeless to begin with, but through consistent practice my mastery did improve. The teachers were compassionate souls who reminded us that whatever stage of yogic practice we were at, it was perfect. I remember an expression one particular instructor used frequently: "There is no right or wrong way to practise, there is just practice."

For some reason this phrase spoke to me—spoke to my core essence. There was no expectation to be better, stronger, more flexible or more accomplished than you were. The constant reassurance of "you are enough" was enough for me to enjoy the experience and relax into my practice.

My intuition was persistent, affirming that yoga would be an important part of my forward momentum, of my healing. That it would be an important step on my journey back to self. My intuition was right. So I continued turning up and rolling out my mat in those early days, even on the days I'd have much preferred to shop, drink or indulge in a foot massage. It was my peace and it provided sorely needed relief on the days I wasn't sure I'd even make it through. For the days—so many days—I wasn't sure I was going to survive.

Over the next few months I experimented with different types of yoga, finding Vinyasa to be the most nourishing and beneficial. I found the pace and variety of movement kept my brain and body content to experiment. I had to listen closely to the cues and visually follow the instructor so my body could find its way into the positions. It required concerted focus and effort.

There was also something about the rhythm of movement and strain on my muscles that I found comforting. My quads stretched and my back strengthened. My favourite part of the class was when it was time to stretch out in Savasana, listening to the sound of Tibetan meditation bells or classical music.

I enjoyed developing my skills over those early months, eventually forming a habit; a ritual that sustained me through the daily struggles of existence, the corporate stress and pressure, the pain I was inflicting on my family, and the emotional turmoil Jason's absence from my life was causing me.

I continue to practise once or twice a week and it brings me the same level of comfort and peace as it did in the beginning. Today, my body is stronger and more capable than it has been in decades. I now enjoy the challenge and even the strain. I enjoy how proud I feel when I successfully master a new position or when I feel my muscles flex and move in their new, upgraded ways.

Please don't misunderstand me, I am certainly no yoga guru! Don't ever ask to see any advanced move like a shoulder stand. My downward dog, however, is perfect, I can hold a tree pose for a good minute, and I'm pretty chuffed when the instructor says to flip into wild thing and I manage it without falling over!

I am proud to say I am no longer the woman who slinks into the yoga studio with her head down, in a hurry to lie on her yoga mat and weep. I am now the woman who walks confidently into the studio with my mat under my arm, my head held high and a beaming smile on my face. But this evolution took time. It took discipline and focus and the cultivation of my own internal strength over months and years.

❖

The practice of yoga is now integral to my self-care routine. It challenges me physically, calms me mentally and nourishes me spiritually.

When I exit the studio I feel brighter, more centred, and with an increased ability to cope with whatever life throws at me. It brings objectivity to my thoughts, allows me to process emotions in a more balanced way and invites me to see my life through a broader lens. It is also no longer mandatory, but a deliberate choice I make every week to put me at the heart of myself. At the heart of my healing.

Alcohol

From my first drink of rum and coke at 15 years of age, to the vodka enjoyed as an exchange student in Finland, to the cheap wine and vodka consumed throughout my university days, to the more sophisticated and expensive wines of my 20s, 30s and 40s, alcohol has always played a major role in my social life. Any opportunity to drink was embraced with glee and delight. It's social and it's fun. Until it's not.

It's not something to be proud of but Australians have a global reputation for their ability to drink. There are many segments of society that not only condone alcohol consumption, but forthrightly, emphatically and determinedly encourage it. That's the culture in which I grew up, and alcohol has an energetic charge over me.

In the weeks after meeting Jason, I drank alcohol often and

liberally to numb the feelings of despair, loss and incredulity that I was not already living my life with my soulmate. Indeed, it was the primary destructive tool from my toolbox which I relied on for a long time.

It is no secret in my friendship circles that I have always been a solid drinker. No point in expounding the virtues of moderation to me. I'm all in most of the time. It is not uncommon to polish off a bottle of wine with a friend, then go looking for one more glass to accompany the cheese plate. Often, I wouldn't need the cheese plate as an excuse.

During this time of having my world turned upside down, inside out, and spun round and round, I embraced every opportunity to drink. Before I wandered into my first yoga class, I was enthusiastically committed to my lunchtime drink at a fabulous restaurant with my best friend.

As fortune would have it, we worked for the same company and could easily devise our plans for our lunchtime escape. We didn't indulge every day, but more often than we would both like to admit.

We would talk and drink, drink and talk, sharing intimate details of our lives as only best friends can. It was a safe space for me— a necessity, as I needed a confidant with whom I could rehash every detail of meeting Jason.

I have a foggy memory of one of these lunch escapades. We decided to try the new yum cha restaurant located in a beautiful heritage-listed building not far from the office. It was 2:00 p.m. and I was aching to escape the professional dance my corporate role required. We sat down, and without even looking at the menu, I ordered a bottle of Australian Riesling—a fabulous choice for Chinese cuisine. There was no time to waste—I needed the wine, and I needed it immediately.

We began to plot my new life. The fact Jason and I would be together within weeks was a given, so we went straight into planning mode. I grabbed my journal, which now travelled with me everywhere, and opened my newly created to-do list. The immediate and most pressing issue to discuss was how my husband and I would share care of the children. This discussion raged for a good hour as we were both determined the children would be affected to the least extent possible.

The yum cha trolleys came and went and we feasted on prawn dumplings, duck pancakes, and salt and pepper squid. Although the food was good, the wine was outstanding. We ordered another bottle.

We moved on to the question of where Jason and I would live and what type of house would suit our blended families. That was fun— I remember whipping out my mobile phone and showing her the houses I had been researching. There were so many incredible choices, at a fraction of the cost I had become accustomed to in Sydney, that I could barely hide my delight! Water views—yes, please!!! In my imagination, I was already living my new life with my soulmate. It was already spectacular.

Then we discussed my career, wondering if our company would support my move to another state. If they were not willing to accommodate, we considered other companies I might like to work for. We pondered if there would be suitable roles or if I needed to adjust my expectations of seniority and salary. I was willing to do either, or both.

We staggered out of the restaurant a few hours later, feigning food poisoning so we were not required to re-enter the office environment. In reality, we couldn't. Instead of going home, though, we went to a small, dimly lit local bar. We ordered another bottle of wine. Our tipple of choice this time was an Italian Chianti. Eventually we each took a taxi home, but I don't remember the ride at all.

Of course I knew the drinking wasn't healthy, and it certainly derailed and stalled the work I needed to do to heal myself emotionally, spiritually, mentally and especially physically. It didn't stop me though.

Reading my diary there are plenty of references to being hungover, cancelling appointments or not turning up for work. In fact, after my epic Chinese lunch and subsequent bar excursion, with my state of mind and emotions clearly out of control, I wrote the following diary entry:

It's 9:00 a.m. and I'm back in bed. Yesterday was another huge emotional rollercoaster where too much wine was consumed at lunch to go back to work and the alcohol in my system has made it impossible to stagger into the city today.

I feel dreadful physically—my stomach is nervous, anxious and sick. Emotionally I am distraught. I don't know what to do, what to feel, what my next step is … except sleep. It's all I want to do now.

And just two weeks later …

I was too hungover to work today so I slept and shopped and had lunch and a bottle of wine with Tess. I confided in her about Jason and where my mind was heading with respect to my future. She was lovely and calm and supportive.

Then off I went to Krystyna's and shared a bottle of wine with her and told her all about meeting Jason as well. Again, there was a level of understanding and she was completely supportive of my next move. I have such wonderful friends and they will surely be needed over the next few months.

But oh my God, do I feel dreadful today!!! I don't want to even think about how much I drank yesterday.

I was in so much pain I used alcohol to numb the reality of my life. I turned to alcohol on many occasions over the next few months as I just didn't want to face my life as it was. I didn't want to face a future without Jason. Indeed, it was inconceivable to envisage a future that didn't end in happily ever after with my soulmate. I won't labour my journal entries but there were many, and they make for a confronting read.

The alcohol allowed me to temporarily forget my pain, despair and despondency that set in all too often in the months after meeting Jason. The stinging hangovers and loss of many, many days though had an incredibly detrimental effect on my emotional and physical health.

I would wake up with a searing hangover and swear to myself, NO MORE DRINKING, THAT'S IT!

But you know, after a few days the short-term effects of over-indulgence retreated to the back of my mind—the hangovers would subside, the bruises would heal and the lack of judgement I displayed, although embarrassing, faded from memory. But the pain was still there—ready to rear its ugly head and convince me the only respite was in the bottle of wine.

I'd love to say after those first few months I managed to get my alcohol consumption under control and was on my way to living in perfect health. However, my journey with alcohol wasn't over. In fact, it became a recurring theme. Alcohol was the key detrimental coping mechanism I employed just to keep going.

For now though, it's time to travel to the light side—away from toxins, negativity and self-loathing, and delve into the magical world of music.

Music

I reached out to Jason about a month after we met to let him know that through the circumstances of a family friend's funeral, I would be near his home for a few days. I wrote that it would be lovely to see him. I tried to sound balanced and carefree.

I was desperate to reconnect in person; to see if his feelings for me mirrored my attraction to and feelings for him. Surely they would. I couldn't see it any other way. I couldn't entertain the potential for any other perspective. I wasn't the only one in the energy that night. I wasn't the only one in our intense connection. My eyes were not the only eyes affected. I wasn't the only one in our kisses.

He responded to my email immediately confirming he would love to see me too. I was ecstatic. The emails went back and forth searching for a time that suited us both until ... silence.

The next morning, I received a message. It was brief, unemotive. He had thought about my proposition and decided it wouldn't be a good idea for us to catch up or stay in touch. He declared he didn't want to "mess with my situation". Oh, and as a final sign-off, he said, "Look after yourself." I was devastated.

I couldn't let it go though. As I began to construct the reply, my heart began to pound, my mouth became bone dry, and my body temperature felt like it was spiking above 40 degrees. I wanted to hide. I wanted to disappear. And I also wanted to be sick.

I didn't allow the emotions or physical sensations to stop me. I was brave and I was open, and I showed real vulnerability—and I have never in my life been the vulnerable person in a relationship. I have never in my life shared that level of openness with anyone.

Dear Jason
Okay, I understand and respect your decision.
I had wanted to see you in person, and although a funeral is a terrible reason to get on a plane, I thought the timing—for me at least—was right. It's not ideal to express myself via email, but given your position, I needed to let you know, to give you some insight into the last month for me.
Our encounter in Margaret River, although completely unexpected, was quite overwhelming for me. I am truly grateful to you for our experience. It has given me the opportunity to reexamine how I had been existing in my marriage for some

time, and our experience has given me the courage to act.

This communication comes with no expectation of you. Indeed, I have no insight into your head, your soul, your heart and what—if any—effect our time together had on you.

My husband and I have separated. There is clearly a lot to process and my only goal here is to be completely open and honest. It is important for me to let you know that your role in this was one of catalyst, but again, with no expectation of anything from you.

My feelings developed in such a way during our brief time together that I wanted more. I want my life to be open to new experiences and with time, new love.

He is, to my knowledge, unaware of the part you have played. He was shocked but not surprised at my decision. It had, in truth, been coming for some time. I wasn't ready to share that information with you during our walk, I was just trying to process how my soul was responding and opening to you.

The plans for our future are amicable—the girls come first— and we will work together as a partnership to ensure all their needs are met.

You only live once and I move forward with openness, hope and expectation of an amazing future.

Amanda

I pressed send.
I waited. And I waited. And I waited.

A few days later, having not received a reply, I found myself on a beautiful beach as the sun was rising. Pink and purple painted the sky, and cool, aqua-blue water lapped the shore. It was an extraordinary morning. I had my earphones connected and as my feet hit the sand,

I pressed play on a random Spotify playlist. Diana Ross's incredible song 'I'm Coming Out' filled my ears.

I began to smile and laugh and cry, all at the same time! I actually broke into a spontaneous run. I am no runner! I intuitively and immediately understood the message was meant for me.

My new life was beginning. I was coming out. I didn't know where I was going. I didn't know who would hold my hand, let me cry on their shoulder or let me snuggle into their arms. I didn't know with whom I would enjoy new experiences, travel or solve the world's problems. All I knew that morning as I walked the sand with cool water lapping my feet was that my new life was beginning.

I felt invincible, open, brave and vulnerable. My spirit was soaring, my body was alive. It was one of the most incredible mornings of my life.

After that revelation, 'I'm Coming Out' became my anthem, my theme song, my song that when times were challenging—and there were many—led me home to my soul. It continues to be the most awesome, inspiring, heart-lifting and powerful song in my life. Anytime I play it I receive just as much joy as the first time I really heard it that day on the beach.

The song unfailingly gives me a 'You Go Girl!' vibe. I have integrated the messages that as long as I am positive, that I trust and have faith in myself, then I can make it through life. Not only make it through life but emerge as the real, authentic, flawed, honest and vulnerable Amanda. To confidently step into my power, and let the world see who I truly am.

The emotional trip came to an end a few days later without a phone call, email or text from Jason. I slumped in the airport lounge with my parents and wrote in my journal. I could barely hold back my tears.

I'm at the airport and feeling thoroughly exhausted. It has certainly been a challenging month! Jason didn't contact me— he either doesn't feel the same way about me or doesn't know

how he feels. I desperately wanted to see him. I desperately
wanted to know how he was feeling.

I wanted to understand if he was okay. I desperately wanted
to know if this could be real, if my future really is with him.
I wanted to kiss him and have him hold me and just 'know'.
I wanted that moment in time again, where we looked into
each other's eyes and knew we were home.

I take off for Sydney today, and I have to leave him behind.
I have to be okay with that.

I clearly wasn't okay. I was heartbroken. My soul had been
smashed into a million pieces. But somehow I had to move forward.

Over the next few months I created my very first Spotify playlist,
naming it 'New Life' with 'I'm Coming Out' my first song.

I've always enjoyed music and have it continually playing
throughout my home, and through my headphones whilst out and
about.

In fact, a memory from my youth surfaced that brought a smile to
my eyes. Growing up, like many Australians of my age, I would watch
a music show every Saturday morning that counted down the hits of
the week. I would set up my cassette recorder in front of the TV and
diligently record every song I liked, creating a mixed tape.

This exercise required considerable concentration. I had to ensure
I recorded not only the songs I loved, but started and ended the
recording perfectly. I had to time my bathroom breaks! I would
delight in making these mixed tapes and would play them over and
over again—at least until I would sit in front of the TV a few weeks
later and start the whole process from scratch. A few of my early
favourite songs were Olivia Newton John's 'Let's Get Physical', Kylie
Minogue's 'Locomotion' and 'Karma Chameleon' by Culture Club.
Ha, the memories!

My 'New Life' compilation was much easier (and quicker) to create with a smartphone and Spotify. I would focus on songs of significance to where I was at the time, what I was experiencing, the journey I was now on—the tune, the beat, the lyrics, the memories.

I added holiday anthems like 'Life Is a Rollercoaster' by Ronan Keating as it reminds me of skiing down a Swiss mountain perfecting my parallel turns. I reminisce with a cheeky grin when 'Spinning Around' by Kylie Minogue plays, remembering a New Year's Eve party in Innsbruck with a handsome young Austrian (and yes, he was also tall and dark). And singing 'Freedom' with George Michael (okay, and thousands of others) at an open air concert one Sydney summer!

Songs from my favourite Australian bands INXS and Hunters & Collectors were added for nostalgia, and of course, you couldn't be a girl growing up in the 1980s and 1990s without Madonna as your background frequency.

I didn't always need to search for songs, as some songs found me. I would choose a random Spotify playlist and bam, there it was—a message for me at exactly the time I needed to hear it, just like 'I'm Coming Out'.

Another early addition to my playlist and example of serendipity was Drake's 'Hold on, We're Going Home'.

I grew up close to where Jason lives and always assumed I'd move back home at some point.

In my mind, Sydney was my temporary home in order to enjoy my single days, focus on my career, perhaps meet my husband, perhaps have some children. It is a city where, as a young woman, I could revel in a range of incredible experiences—an orchestral performance at the Sydney Opera House, a Jamiroquai concert in Centennial Park, a drive to Palm Beach to savour lunch at an amazing waterfront restaurant, or immerse myself in the diverse cultural events the city hosted throughout the year.

But I never felt it was my long-term home or where I truly belonged. My spiritual home has never left me, it has always called me back.

Meeting Jason was obviously universal alignment on my journey. It was a clear sign it was time to move back and of course, be with Jason.

'Hold On, We're Going Home' was almost perfect; I just changed a few lyrics to suit my purpose so it became 'Hold On, I'm Coming Home'.

Another song that became critical to my healing was the theme song from the TV series *Revenge*. It was Rachel Platten's 'Fight Song'. It is incredibly empowering! I integrated the messages that you must believe in yourself and honour yourself, even in the face of strong adversity. Regardless of what anyone else thinks, your life is worth fighting for.

So fight I did.

As the months dragged on without any communication with Jason the song served as a constant reminder to take back my own power. To believe I was enough. To believe I was worthy. To become my own hero. If I could survive meeting my soulmate and not enjoy my happily ever after with him, I could survive anything. If you haven't heard 'Fight Song', go find it and play it. It may just change the way you view yourself, the way you respect yourself and the way you move yourself forward in the world—one step at a time.

There came a time that some songs on my original playlist no longer served me; instead, they hurt me. By the time I really faced the fact that Jason and I would not be together, some songs only reminded me of him, and that brought my spirit, energy and enthusiasm for life crashing down.

It was clearly time to create a new playlist. Introducing 'I Am Woman'.

Some songs made it from 'New Life.' Of course, 'I'm Coming Out' was mandatory, as was 'Fight Song', but others just had to go. I vividly remember my finger hovering and hesitating over the delete button of 'Hold On, We're Going Home'. I argued over and over with

31

myself as I really didn't want to let it (him) go. But the song was a constant reminder of the fantasy life I had imagined and my dream had not manifested. In order to create a soundtrack for the new life I was creating, it had to go. I pressed delete. I gave myself permission to cry.

New additions supported my emotional, spiritual and physical strength, my continued personal growth and my forward motion.

'I Will Survive' by Gloria Gaynor reminds me that I am a powerful, triumphant woman capable of taking on any challenge; 'Broken Arrows' by Avicii (rest in peace, incredible soul) never fails to lift my spirits when I become despondent; and 'Flames' by David Guetta and Sia reminds me to just keep moving and focus firmly on the future. I also love 'You Can't Hurry Love' by The Supremes—the reason is obvious!

My choice of music can vary from day to day, and sometimes hour to hour. I surrender and go with what works, and it works. Michael Jackson comes on the radio and my feet start grooving and my hips start swaying. I am thoroughly present, engaged and joyful in that moment! Music soothes my soul and facilitates healing in so many ways; I feel incredibly blessed to experience the sound of music (favourite movie of all time—just sayin') in my life.

For me, dancing is a nourishing and delightful accompaniment to music. It has been a valuable outlet for the release of stress and tension all my life. From the early days of nightclubbing with my cousins on the Gold Coast where I'd spend hours carving up the dancefloor, to dancing at home with the girls (or by myself!) when the mood strikes for a boogie, to being silly with girlfriends on weekends away.

I remember a hilarious evening whilst on a wine weekend where, after a full day of sampling the best the Clare Valley had to offer, we ordered pizza and cracked a few bottles of pinot noir. When the pizza was finished, we channelled Madonna's greatest vogue moves on top of the dining table! We also recreated the Macarena as a foursome—and it was a miracle we didn't fall off the table (or to be honest, break it!).

I can be adventurous and clumsy when I shake my booty and although I grossly overestimate my grooviness, I don't give a damn. When you bypass your rational mind, your self-consciousness disappears, leaving you free to explore your soul. That's when the magic of inner connection happens. And it's to be honoured and celebrated.

Travelling

Barely a week after letting my husband know our marriage was over, the family holiday to Bali that was pre-planned, pre-booked and pre-paid was upon us.

I offered to stay home but we decided, together, we would both go. The girls were overly excited, and we were travelling with two families who were good friends, and in our crew in the neighbourhood. One couple was aware of the separation, but we hadn't even had the chance to let the second family in on the news before our adventure began. It had only been five weeks since I met Jason. It felt like a lifetime.

We spent the first few days wandering the streets of Ubud, known as the spiritual centre of Bali. Ubud is high in the mountains, surrounded by rainforest and blessed with spectacular terraced rice paddy fields. Hindu temples and shrines glisten in the rising sun and the extraordinary natural environment soothes most souls. The contrast between my internal world and the external environment though could not have been further apart. Internally my heart and my soul were breaking.

Whilst resting from the heat by the pool one afternoon, surrounded by gorgeous frangipani trees, I was reminded of one of my favourite movies that was filmed in Ubud—*Eat, Pray, Love*. It is based on Elizabeth Gilbert's inspiring book of the same name. Her story suddenly became much more significant to me. I recognised in that moment that although Liz may have come into her awakening in a different way, her journey to find her true self resonated deeply and personally with me. It led to an immense appreciation and infinite admiration for the souls who have navigated the waters of heartbreak and loss and made it through to the other side—happier and more satisfied with life. I exhaled.

We would spend the mornings brunching on delicious pastries, indulge in sublime beauty treatments during the day, and spend the afternoons lounging by the pool watching the kids swim and squeal with delight. Then came the biggest decision of the day—which incredible restaurant would we frequent for an evening of authentic Balinese cuisine, or Mexican if it was kids' choice! It was luxurious, it was decadent and for most, it was joyful.

Underneath my smiley façade, I was screaming, I was crumbling, I was breaking apart. I didn't know where to go or what to think. When I couldn't find the energy to keep my smiley face on, I was grumpy and snappy. I would spend long periods of time away from the fun and festivities of the group, escaping to the beach for a walk and a cry. I needed to release the escalating tension from my body, and I certainly didn't need to be reminded that some couples were happy and content with each other.

I also endured heated discussions on asset splits and child custody arrangements with my husband. There were many, many tears. I spent a lot of time alone in bed. It was certainly not the holiday we had planned mere months earlier.

Somehow though, through all the pain and turmoil, I managed to remain optimistic about my future life with Jason. I still couldn't understand how we could have experienced our connection and not fallen into each other's arms immediately and forever. I still wasn't willing to accept the possibility of any other outcome.

I replayed the experience of our morning in my mind over and over again. Where he asked me in all sincerity as he held my hand in his, "What's the solution here? What are we going to do?"

I had just moved the biggest obstacle to us being together, yet there had been no further communication between us.

Everything changed the afternoon we returned from Bali. I walked into the house and turned on my work phone. I scrolled through the hundreds of emails that had arrived whilst away—you sometimes forget the world doesn't stop spinning when you take a precious and crucial break from work.

Hidden amongst the client correspondence and macroeconomic updates was his reply. It was sent two weeks after I sent my email, where I daringly shared my most intimate feelings—where I confessed I had separated from my husband, opening the door to a future together.

I retreated to the master bedroom to read his response. I read it once, I read it twice. I had to concentrate on breathing.

It was brief, unemotive, dismissive. It was a no.

He had deliberately decided to let our connection rest, to release the energetic bond between us, to move forward in his life without looking back.

I just couldn't understand it. His email read as if he wasn't even there. Wasn't he in our experience? Did he not share the energy? He told me to focus on my health and fitness, and to stay positive, open and honest. He then added "we could all be dead tomorrow, so always have something to look forward to".

I didn't even know how to begin to assimilate this message, let alone the tone in which it had been sent. I was floored and confused, utterly perplexed and physically exhausted. I was also heartbroken.

It made me doubt all over again.

Was it just me? Was I delusional when I reflected on our many conversations where our repertoire flowed as naturally as water in a stream? Was the physicality of our responses to each other only in my mind? Did I imagine the intensity of connection through our eyes? Was our kiss, where it felt like the most natural connection in the world—where it felt like coming home for the first time in my life— just a figment of my imagination? Was I in an alternate reality when my soul was woken from a lifetime of slumber? When I experienced the feeling of absolute knowing, just knowing?

No. He was there. He experienced the connection. He felt the energy. He experienced us. He saw me through his eyes as clearly as I saw him through mine. But he chose to dismiss it. To fight it. To move ahead without turning back. He chose to give away what may have been the most incredible soul-fulfilling connection of this lifetime. But he has that choice. He has free will and he exercised it.

But why? Why? I've agonised over this question for far too many hours on this journey and I always reach the same heartbreaking conclusion—I may never know.

My evening diary entry:

The universe delivered a deep, loving soul connection in Jason. Had our connection not been as powerful and electric as it was, I probably would have dismissed or ignored it. I could have dismissed it as a lovely evening of flirtation and that was it. Instead, he was sent to me in his tall, dark and irresistibly handsome package for me to make the changes required for my future.

Now to the future. I summon all my courage and my strength to disentangle myself from the life I have with my husband in a calm and loving way. To sell the house and establish a new, comfortable and safe home for the girls and me.

I need to accept the transition from being part of a couple to being single again will be extremely uncomfortable and distressing for a time but necessary for my future and the happiness of all concerned (not just me).

I need to focus on my physical health and prioritise my emotional well-being. The ultimate goal is to move forward positively and win at this adventure called LIFE. I have to do this. And I have to do this alone—without Jason by my side or even in my life.

I have to keep a laser focus on the tasks ahead, holding true in the knowledge I will experience joy, soul connection, intimate compatibility and emotional commitment with the right man who will appear at exactly the right time and at the right stage of his evolution to embrace me, to embrace us.

It isn't going to be Jason. I need to say goodbye. I need to come back to self.

So that is what I did.

But it was far from easy. It wasn't smooth sailing; it wasn't all growth and forward movement and peaches with cream. The real work, the journey back to me was, in reality, only just beginning.

3.
Discovering Spirituality

I am known, as I am knowing ...

A year or so before meeting Jason I asked the universe that if it was the best outcome for all involved, to put someone tall, dark and handsome in front of me that made it absolutely clear I should leave my husband.

I can't explain where the thought came from, I just trusted it was the right thought to have. It was also so specific I didn't have any expectation of the universe delivering on my request.

So why did I feel the need to put the thought into the universe in the first place?

A few years after the birth of our second child I began to accept there would be a time in the future when my husband and I would no longer be together. I loved him, and certainly did when I said my vows, but in my core, I began to feel it wasn't forever.

That's extremely hard to admit, even now. I think we all have expectations that the person we marry—if we are lucky enough to have free choice in the first place—will be our partner and be by our side for the rest of our lives. I did. And I held and cherished that belief for many years.

Over time, with personal growth and our ambitions and outlook on life continually adjusting, the doubts began to surface. But it was comfortable, and we were content. We didn't fight. We had a good partnership. We had two gorgeous children and extremely busy careers. I had also grown up in a traditional nuclear family and felt the weight of societal and parental expectations to maintain a 'happy family'.

Of course, Mr Tall, Dark and Handsome was introduced in the most unexpected of circumstances, in the most unlikely of locations, and my life changed forever.

It did get me thinking of the request I put out there. Was there any conceivable chance the universe actually did have something to do with my meeting Jason? Meeting Jason at a time I would be open to the possibility of another life trajectory? A life path that was different to the disciplined and somewhat predictable one I was on?

I pondered further questions. Was it feasible that a greater force was pulling the strings in my human existence? Were we actually at the hands of universal destiny, irrespective of what our ego and willpower desired for our life? Was it possible to not only connect with the universe, but to be heard? Not only heard, but have desires manifest in real life?

The thought that you can manifest into your life a person, an event, an experience certainly gave me much to consider. I'm not talking about the Law of Attraction here, I'm talking about a dialogue with the universe where you are open to possibilities that seem, at the time, actually impossible. Even downright ridiculous. There, I said it! (You were probably thinking it!)

So, it begs the question: how does one dialogue with the universe?

The most common is through prayer. Religion is the most universally understood context for prayer and it is how I identified with a greater presence my whole life.

I was born and raised in the Catholic faith, attended church regularly until 18 years of age, attended an all-girls Catholic boarding school, then lived at an all-girls Catholic college at university. My father still practises weekly and is devoted to his faith. I am in awe of his dedication and service.

For many people all over the world religious prayer is a beautiful, powerful way to connect with the divine, with God. But the traditional religious trajectory is not the path I am now on. I am now firmly on the spiritual path.

Physical Shock

I had been feeling lethargic and drained of energy for some time (realistically, it had been years) and I was on the hunt for answers. I had two small children and a full-time career, so those lifestyle factors clearly had an impact on my health. I was also carrying extra weight so there was a visually obvious reason for my lethargic state. My appetite had always been healthy, but I wasn't a junk food consumer. I would maybe have fast food once or twice a year—usually on long road trips where fast food was the only option.

I am extremely partial to cheese and crackers (with a liberal pouring of pinot noir) and I relish a good restaurant meal. I am also a competent cook, cooking from scratch most of the time. My portions are generous but even so, I would often be the first back to the kitchen to indulge in second helpings. I had the "there are starving children in Africa" line from my childhood in the 1980s on constant mental replay. But instinctively I knew there was more going on with my health, and I was right. Hmmm, maybe I was plugged into the universe after all—I just wasn't listening most of the time.

Not long before meeting Jason I had a hair mineral analysis conducted to get a better understanding of my lethargy. This is a non-invasive test that utilises a hair sample to assess nutrient and toxic elements in body tissue. Minerals in the correct balance play a crucial role in the body's ability to grow, heal and thrive but when they are out of balance they can wreak havoc on your whole system.

The results of the hair mineral analysis were diabolical, and you certainly don't need a laundry list of my ailments. However, one important discovery was that an off-the-charts high copper load was affecting my energy and the absorption of nutrients. A recommended protocol to correct this particular imbalance was the regular use of an infrared sauna. Infrared saunas are proven to reduce an accumulated toxic overload over time, allowing the body to facilitate its own healing. I was exceedingly open to any protocol that would help heal my body and restore much-needed energy, so I purchased a sauna and began the experiment.

My infrared sauna is a solo sauna where you lie on a base mat and pull the dome cover all the way to your neck so only your head is out of the cocoon(or coffin, as my friends lovingly refer to it!). The best way to describe it—it's like a tanning bed. The dome and mat heats your body until your pores break with sweat, thus releasing toxins out of the body through your skin. Voila, adios copper!

However, I quickly realised it afforded another incredible benefit. It mandated I stop and take a little time for myself a couple of times a week and I enthusiastically embraced it! Once in the sauna, there was nowhere to go and no one to be with, except myself.

Before I met Jason, I would put on some music, jump in and spend the time compiling a mental list of jobs to complete when the sauna finished. After I met Jason, my focus completely changed. I found myself spending that 'me' time feverishly seeking answers to a seemingly never-ending stream of questions.

What the hell had I just experienced? How do I process my reaction to him emotionally? How do I process this physically? What don't I understand? How do I move through this? Am I actually insane? Will I even survive this experience? Oh, and did I remember to buy the organic fruit snacks for the kids' lunchboxes?!

It was my relentless search for answers that led me to arguably the most important resource for my journey thus far—it led me to Hay House, a company dedicated to supporting positive change in the world. Hay House quickly became my go-to destination for answers to my innumerable questions. It became the gateway, the bridge to begin to learn the language of spirituality. For the first time since meeting Jason I felt I was understanding—something. I started to breathe, and to believe I wasn't insane.

There was a whole universe of knowledge I had never been exposed to, nor tapped into. A whole universe of love, support and education awaiting my consumption. This support came from incredibly talented, heart-centred and influential authors, thought leaders and creatives.

And it all started in my sauna!

I was listening to Hay House radio during my evening session. I chose a meditative healing of the body exercise. I can't remember who facilitated the session, but boy oh boy, do I remember the way the evening changed me physically. I had no expectations, I was really just looking for an escape from my endless thoughts of Jason and was guided to find a practice that might calm my nerves and centre me in my body. I lay in my sauna and pressed play.

The tingling sensation, like pins and needles, started in my feet. It was a strange feeling, but I embraced it.

But the pins and needles didn't restrict themselves to my feet. They made their way up my body. All. The. Way. Up. Within minutes my whole body was buzzing. Relaxed and accepting to begin with, I soon became concerned at the escalation of the energetic frequency pulsing through me.

The intensity of the sensations continued to increase. My intuition instructed me to flex my legs. I tried, but I couldn't feel them. I then realised with alarm I couldn't move them. They were paralysed. I checked my torso. Nope, I couldn't feel it, I couldn't move my chest. I checked my arms and found them immobile. My hands and fingers contorted into the most unnatural of shapes and just ... froze. I couldn't move any part of my body. I was completely paralysed. It was (almost) unbelievable.

I checked in mentally—had I fallen asleep? No. Was I dreaming? No. I was awake and aware and now, completely petrified.

I couldn't speak. I couldn't call for help. Not even a whisper would escape my throat. I fought the panic rising in me. I fought the fear that was becoming so intense it threatened to overwhelm me. I lay on the mat with my body paralysed, my hands and fingers contorted, and my jaw locked for what seemed like forever. I realised urgently I had only one job at that moment—to breathe.

Then I did the only thing left to do: I surrendered. I surrendered to the universe. I had to. I couldn't do anything else. I allowed the energy—the terrifyingly intense pins and needles—to rock and roll through my body. I closed my eyes and concentrated on every breath, ensuring air continued to move into and out of my lungs. I focused, only, on living.

The pins and needles eventually began decreasing in their intensity. I'm not sure how long this took as the sauna had long since switched itself off. I found the courage, through the still-elevated sense of panic in my chest, to attempt movement. With immense relief I felt my body slowly but surely respond. I wiggled my toes and my feet came back to life. The unnatural shapes of my hands and fingers began to release. A few minutes later my jaw began to unlock. I yawned.

I lay on the mat until my body released all the energy. This took a good half hour, perhaps longer; I had no concept of time. When I felt ready, I peeled myself off the floor, thoroughly depleted. I was overwhelmed with emotion. I cried and I cried. Then I fell into the deepest sleep I had enjoyed for many years.

I didn't speak to anyone about this experience as it seemed so surreal and implausible; I just didn't think I could articulate what happened to my body without sounding crazy.

I look back now and have immense gratitude for that beyond frightening evening. The unhealthy, stuck energy—a consequence of the rigidity of how I had lived my life up to that point—had been unlocked and removed from my body. It had been transformed and transmuted. That experience was the catalyst to begin my physical healing—discharging the unconscious stress and tension I had carried all my life. This was my introduction to greater universal energy. Certainly unique. Absolutely unforgettable!

In the weeks that followed I was overwhelmingly anxious about the prospect of another sauna session—would I have to endure another round of paralysis? Could I actually subject myself to that again? My conscious mind was slowly beginning to entertain the notion that the experience may have been for my highest good, so one night I took a few deep breaths, chose an orchestral piece of music, and jumped in. My session that evening was calming for my emotions, nourishing for my soul and thankfully paralysis-free for my body. I exhaled.

Conscious Gratitude

Gratitude is a word often overused in the day to day but rarely given the credence and honour it deserves. It is a concept many children are introduced to with something like: "You should be grateful you have a roof over your head, food on the table and a bed to sleep in." And that's completely true and completely valid. As an Australian kid from a middle-class household, who knew no other way of growing up, being grateful for what I already had wasn't—in my mind anyway—necessary.

I am acutely aware that my experience is incredibly trivial compared to the inequalities and injustices that exist the world over. Even writing these words now, I cringe in embarrassment at my 'distress'. I have had to move forward in life without my soulmate by my side, sure, but that's hardly comparable to going without clean water or food, the overwhelming anxiety of homelessness, being a victim of any type of violence, suffering chronic ill-health, having to leave one's own country never able to return, or any other misfortune souls endure on a daily basis on this planet.

So when did the concept of conscious gratitude enter my life?

It's only with age, and by taking time to reflect have I become keenly aware of my fortune. Sure, things haven't always been great and haven't always gone to my plan, but I never suffered, nor was

I ever denied anything I needed to survive. My basic physiological needs of food, water, warmth, rest, security and safety were never in jeopardy. Nor were my psychological needs of esteem, belonging and love ever absent from my life. Oh wow, have I been blessed. Oh wow, have I been spoiled. Oh wow, have I been privileged.

The most fortunate are those who have a
wonderful capacity to appreciate,
again and again, freshly and naively,
the basic goods of life with awe,
pleasure, wonder and even ecstasy
Abraham Maslow

So now, every day and in any way, I consciously find an avenue to express my gratitude. It's an intentional thought I cultivate and say "thank you" in my mind; I write what I am grateful for in my journal, I express to friends how fortunate I am to have them in my life, I sit in quiet contemplation and tears begin to fall down my cheeks in recognition of my many blessings, and I make a point to contribute in a material way that tangibly benefits others.

This practice of conscious gratitude grounds awareness of my fortune leaving me feeling lighter in body and soul. I also feel more satisfied with life, enjoy elevated levels of happiness and can draw on a greater foundation of resilience when faced with the challenges life continues to throw my way. What an incredible gift.

Acknowledging the good that you already have in your
life is the foundation for all abundance
Eckhart Tolle

Gratitude also provides a feeling of alignment with my higher self. A reminder that Spirit is constantly with me, encouraging me and cheering me on. I am incredibly humbled to have a journey at all. I move forward with an immense appreciation for the life I have been gifted, and I am determined to make the most of every day and of every opportunity afforded me. It's the very least I can do.

It took time, but I decided to look at my experience of meeting Jason through the lens of gratitude, and wholeheartedly believe this has been beneficial for my emotional health. If it were not for our encounter in Margaret River, I may not have chosen to do the hard work of going within.

If I hadn't gone within, would I have made the drastic changes required to course correct a life that was not aligned with who I am meant to be in this lifetime? Maybe, but in all honesty, I probably wouldn't have. Life was good—my relationship with my husband worked, my job worked, my friendships worked, my family worked, my children were happy.

It has taken a considerable amount of time alone and many, many tears to recognise this, but I wasn't happy. I am truly grateful for meeting Jason for shaking me out of my unconscious state of sadness, my unconscious deep longing for a different experience in this lifetime, and so much more.

Darling Girl

I have two wonderful, gorgeous daughters whom I love to the moon and back. They are both precious and unique, unequivocally worthy of love. Since the day they were born I've addressed them both as "darling girl". The adoration conveyed via these words has created a beautiful bond of emotional closeness between us. I've also witnessed how it has helped them to cultivate a sense of confidence and self-love that many full-grown women struggle to create for themselves— me included.

These two gifts have in so many ways saved my life over the past few years. They gave me a focus beyond myself as they needed and demanded my attention. As was their right!

I had to redirect my limited energy from my internal, all-consuming grief to ensure they were well fed and watered. At times it was all I was capable of. I used to joke that they were still alive when I returned them to their father. Luckily for me he managed to retain his sense of humour!

During this time of trying to balance the emotional needs of the girls—where my guilt was all-encompassing given it was me who inflicted the emotional pain—I was not kind or easy on myself.

In the months after meeting Jason I engaged in an unending stream of targeted emotional abuse, torturing myself with all the questions: Why hasn't he contacted me? What's wrong with me? What is he thinking? How is he feeling? What's wrong with me? What is he doing? Why hasn't he recognised our connection? What's wrong with me? Was it a mistake to send the email? Why hasn't he responded? What's WRONG with me? You get my drift.

I engaged in such negative self-talk I could barely look at myself, let alone look at myself with any measure of compassion or love. I would utter phrases under my breath (and out loud!) like *"I'm not good enough"*, *"I'm not attractive enough"*, *"I'm too old for him"* most days as it was obviously my fault I had lost him. I had, somehow, sabotaged our connection.

And then one day, with the help of Louise Hay and her famous mirror work teachings, I looked at myself. I mean, I really looked at myself: in the mirror. Into my own eyes. I had been avoiding me for such a long time, I didn't know what I really looked like.

> *Mirror work is the most effective method I've found for learning to love yourself and see the world as a safe and loving place. I have been teaching people how to do mirror work for as long as I have been teaching affirmations*
> **Louise L. Hay**

Mirror work encourages you to learn to love yourself, as you are, every day. The ultimate goal is to connect with and soothe your inner child. An inner child who has likely been neglected for many years. The basis of Louise's teaching is that affirmations affect your subconscious and these affirmations establish, over time, habitual ways of thinking and behaving.

It was time to have a good, hard discussion with myself about my internal dialogue! Perhaps it was time to actively plant seeds of confidence, self-esteem, self-love and internal peace? Perhaps it was time to give myself a damn break.

So how did this experiment with mirror work unfold for me?

It began one morning in my apartment. While most were out enjoying a glorious warm Sydney day, I instead stood in front of my bathroom mirror. I took some deep breaths, steeled myself, and for the first time in many, many years, sought out my own eyes. I stood in complete silence as I held my gaze. I felt uncomfortable. I felt foolish. Yet I persisted.

The physical sensations came first. I felt my breath constrict in my throat to the point I had to consciously concentrate on breathing. I persisted. I then felt my heart palpitations increase to the point I thought my heart would jump right out of my chest. I persisted. I stared deeply into my own eyes, through excruciating discomfort and immense embarrassment, although I was clearly alone.

Then it happened: I saw through the mask I had been wearing for so many years. I cracked the wall I had built that kept me from myself. I saw myself—my true essence. I connected with my soul. I started crying until I could hold my gaze no longer. I covered my eyes with the palms of my hands, shaking my head with both incredulity and relief. I left the bathroom and sat on the edge of my bed, recognising my trembling legs were not going to support my weight much longer.

As I reflect on this experience, tears are again welling in my eyes and my breathing is challenged like it was that day. I remember it so vividly—the day it dawned on me, the day of my profound revelation. I am my own "darling girl". I am unequivocally worthy of love.

Now, with no trepidation and no level of discomfort, this is how I speak to myself: sweetheart, darling girl, darling, gorgeous.

No word is too flowery or appreciative, no word is too over the top or too flattering. I speak to myself in a calm and kind way and it fills me with faith, determination and resilience. It fills me with love— love for myself.

It's not always easy and it doesn't always come naturally. There are many times I am disconnected and neither kind to myself, nor forgiving of myself. This is usually when I am stressed and not coping—when work is too intense, the girls' behaviour is challenging, a friendship is off-course, financial challenges are present or when I am just too tired for self-care. I am a work in progress and probably always will be.

I find that when I am grounded, in my body and in my heart, I can make the intimate connection with my soul through the exploration of my own eyes. I am then complete; I am then at peace. It doesn't matter if I'm having a good or bad hair day or carrying extra kilos, if I am hungover, anxious, restless, melancholy or enduring a skin breakout thanks to my overindulgence of chocolate. I can come back to myself and appreciate and love myself exactly as I am, at any point in time.

To come through this experience, when there were so many times I didn't think my human body would make it, and emerge from the ashes like a phoenix rising (I am a Scorpio, after all), it feels like a miracle. I am so grateful I found tools that gave me the strength to persist.

The Angelic Realms

Whilst surfing the Hay House website, hungry for knowledge and continued spiritual development, I came across the online courses.

I was drawn to Kyle Gray's 'Connecting With the Angels Made Easy' and immediately signed up.

This was my first real introduction to angels outside of traditional religious teachings, and I was curious to learn. Did they really exist? If so, what can they teach us? How can they guide us? How can they support us? How does one even begin to work with them? Tell me more!

My thirst for spiritual knowledge was insatiable and I was eager to first understand, then implement any practice that would expedite my healing to move me away from my incredible all-consuming pain and grief to a lighter space of understanding and perhaps, even acceptance. Acceptance that there could be a higher purpose for meeting Jason other than to fall head over heels in love, be together every day and live in soulmate bliss for the rest of our lives.

Kyle Gray—perhaps an unlikely guide with his shaved head, eyebrow ring, arms crammed with tattoos and a thick Scottish accent—turned out to be just the man to introduce me to the concept of angels. He straightforwardly explained that angels have been known by many names in different cultures, belief systems and religions through the ages.

They are known as ancestral beings in many Indigenous traditions, as kami in the Japanese Shinto religion, as bodhisattva in Tibetan Buddhism, as star ancestors in some Native American tribes, as winged Isis in ancient Egypt, as devas in Hinduism, the malaikah in Islam, and in Judaism and Christianity they are called angels. Though cultural descriptions and beliefs vary, the simple definition is that they are pure, divine spiritual beings. They are energy and they are always with us.

It is Kyle's belief that there is a hierarchy of angels who carry out different roles in the spiritual and earthly realms. The archangels are the boss angels (think Archangel Michael, Archangel Uriel, Archangel Gabriel) who look after the earth, its inhabitants, one's journey of spiritual growth and who are in charge of the guardian angels.

Our guardian angels have been dedicated to us since birth, and are with us at all times. They help us out, cheer us on and are best able to directly support us. While this is just one interpretation of the angelic realms, it is definitely one that clicked for me.

For most of my life I have been an angel sceptic: rolling my eyes in disbelief and feeling a sense of sorrow for the poor souls who actually thought angels existed. I would politely listen and smile if someone professed to know for certain that there was an unseen force for good, peace and love guiding and protecting us mere mortals on this earthly realm.

During these discussions I felt more than a little incredulous, more than a little bored and snickered more than once. That is me no more.

Make yourself familiar with the angels,
and behold them frequently in spirit;
for, without being seen, they are present with you
St Francis of Sales

At this time in my life I was in such acute pain, so desperate for any skerrick of relief and for any sense that I was part of something bigger than myself that I decided, "What the hell, let's give it a go." I was in my darkened bedroom, lying on my bed under a light throw when I began my experiment. I closed my eyes, emptied my mind to the best of my ability and simply concentrated on my breath.

The advice was to ask for help as divine beings do not assist without your free will request. So I opened with, "Hello, angels, I would like some help. What do I need to know?" I lay there waiting, wondering if and how any answers would come through. Would I be answered by the angelic realms or would my mind concoct a response to placate me? I didn't know. But I released the scepticism that threatened to derail my experiment and opened myself up to trust.

Almost immediately I sensed it would be okay. Feelings of peace and calm enveloped me, surrounding my body. I would say it was more intuition than anything else. I didn't know how it would all work out—they certainly were not letting me in on that secret!—but

I intuitively knew it would. I felt guided and protected. That initial experience gave me the confidence to open my mind and my heart to the practice of conversing with the angelic realms.

Whenever a friend asks me about my relationship with the angelic realms, I tell this story. It's not wild or earth-shattering; there were no lightning bolts or big, deep, commanding voices from the great beyond, just an intuitive knowing. An intuitive sense of love and support. And that is enough for me.

I am still a novice. I engage where I feel most comfortable—with my guardian angels and the archangels. I sometimes speak to the angels out loud (usually when I'm alone!), I sometimes look towards the sky when I am conversing with the angels and sometimes I just thank them for their assistance in my mind.

I am calmer, and more centred and connected than I have ever been. I exist in a space with unquestionable faith that I do not tread this world alone. I innately and intuitively understand I have help and support available from the angelic realms whenever I ask for it. Conversing with my angelic team is now second nature to me and there are days in my week where they are the only beings I speak to. And I am more than okay with that.

Divination

I have Doreen Virtue and Colette Baron-Reid to thank for my introduction to the world of oracle cards. I owe a debt of gratitude to these incredible women for sharing their knowledge, devotion and passion for this medium of communing with Spirit.

This tangible way of conversing with the universe has enhanced and supported my spiritual growth in remarkable ways. It has been thought-provoking, comforting and even heartbreaking, but ultimately it has been a trusted channel to support me through the experience of meeting my soulmate.

The history and origin of oracle cards is not uniform (at least according to my research), so I won't delve into it too much here. They became popular in the early 1900s in Europe with the advent of the Lenormand Oracle and then gained broader, more global popularity from the 1970s. In simple terms, oracle cards can help navigate life from a place of uncertainty to one of knowing. This form of divination has allowed me to make choices from a place of inspired wisdom, increasing my confidence in my ability to direct my own life.

This experiment wasn't without its challenges. In the early days I had to consciously and determinedly suspend my disbelief in order to trust the guidance I received.

I read somewhere that if you consider oracle cards as the steering wheel of your car—a fabulous tool to guide you to your correct destination—then you can relax into the practice. That tangible analogy certainly helped me.

My experiences have been miraculous. Not that every reading was positive and affirming of my life ahead (in my mind the only way forward was with Jason by my side until death did us part), but they have always been instructive and ultimately, truthful. Source will not lie. It can't. It's not the deal. The deal is to provide accurate guidance and deliver the messages that need to be received. The trick on this side of the veil is to make sure that we always ask for the best possible option to be revealed, the 'this or something better' that serves the highest good of all. This is sometimes easier said than done.

In the early days of reading the cards, either physically or via apps, if I didn't like the message, I would simply delete it. I didn't want to receive 'no', 'not now' or 'not for you'. Nor was I interested in any messages sent to protect me. I only wanted the positive affirmations that I was on the right track and that my soulmate and I would be living in ecstasy together any moment, thank you very much!

However, slowly (agonisingly slowly), as my understanding and appreciation of communing with Spirit via oracle cards matured, I began to recognise that it was in my highest good, and the highest good of all to accept these messages as well. Let's just say it took me some time to get on board with that way of thinking.

I conducted my first reading the day I returned home from Margaret River using my Archangel Oracle deck by Doreen Virtue. I was desperate for answers and intuitively knew I needed to connect with myself. Maybe it was a stroke of genius or maybe I was just listening to my intuition for the first time in a very long time (or perhaps a nudge from my own guardian angels), but I picked up the deck gifted to me by my dear friend Krystyna.

I asked my angels (that's what the instructions said to do) the only question that consumed me: *Is Jason my soulmate?*

I held this question inside my heart and inside my soul and shuffled the deck. One of the more popular spreads is to choose three cards, so I did. These were my very first archangel oracle messages:

BELOVED ONE – ARCHANGEL CHAMUEL
"I am helping you with your Spiritual Soulmate Relationship."

COMPASSION – ARCHANGEL ZADKIEL
"Soften your heart with respect to this situation, and all the people involved, including yourself."

DIVINE ORDER – ARCHANGEL RAGUEL
"Everything is how it needs to be right now. Look past the illusion, and see the underlying order."

Reading the very first message from Archangel Chamuel rendered me speechless. My heart almost stopped beating. It was incredibly confronting. It was (almost) unbelievable. As I relaxed into the message though, I intuitively knew it to be true. My imagination wasn't out of control. I wasn't insane. I wasn't in some elaborate universal plot to break me open and tear me down. Jason was the one. Jason was my soulmate.

I felt it in my heart on the morning of our walk. I felt it in the calmness that washed over me as we sat side by side in our delicious bubble of soul recognition. I felt it in the intimacy and astonishing familiarity of our kisses. I felt it and I knew it that cool and crisp morning as we looked deeply into each other's eyes.

Until then, I thought the idea of a soulmate was a fanciful concept that kept the movie studios and romance books in business. It certainly didn't happen to ordinary folk, certainly didn't happen in real life and it certainly wasn't going to happen to someone like me. Surely, I couldn't be that lucky?

The next piece of advice delivered by Archangel Zadkiel was to have compassion as this situation was going to change many people's lives as well as my own. I was being subtly prepared for my next chapter in recognition there would be pain, sadness, despair, anger and loss in the lives of those I cared most for in this world. I was also advised to approach the situation with a loving heart. If I could manage this, creative solutions benefiting all would be found.

It also reminded me to compassionately consider Jason's point of view. It was then it dawned on me: I didn't honestly know anything about how he was living his life, or if someone was already in his life. I didn't ask that morning. I knew he wasn't married, so I reasoned I was the problem with moving us forward, not him.

My last message was from Archangel Raguel. It provided, even in the most profound and tumultuous time, some peace. It allowed me to begin the process of surrender. If I could recognise and accept that all was as it was meant to be at that moment, if I had faith and held love at the core of the situation, and if I kept my thoughts and spirits high, I would find the strength to move through this experience.

Breathe. Breathe and trust. Breathe and love.

A few weeks later, as my conviction to leave my marriage accelerated, I consulted my archangel cards again. I was understanding more clearly how to work with the oracle cards and asked a more evolved question: *In my highest good, and for the highest good of all, what are the key messages I need to receive now?*

I received the following guidance:

COMPASSION – ARCHANGEL ZADKIEL
"Soften your heart with respect to this situation, and all the people involved, including yourself." Again.

HEALTHY LIFESTYLE – ARCHANGEL RAPHAEL
"Eat a healthful diet, get adequate sleep, and exercise regularly for optimal health."

COURAGE – ARCHANGEL ARIEL
"Be courageous, and stand up for your beliefs."

Ummm, wow, again. These messages felt completely aligned. Archangel Zadkiel appeared again, reminding me to approach the situation with both compassion and forgiveness for all involved. I was acutely aware of the devastation my decision would have on those dearest to me. But I also knew that if I was to survive this, I needed to find a way to also forgive myself. It was another ah-ha moment.

Archangel Raphael then came to me, gently nudging me to prioritise my physical health and well-being in recognition that strong levels of energy and an adequate level of self-esteem would be crucial as I transitioned to my new life. Hmmm, how's that brie and bottle of pinot noir tasting now?

Finally, Archangel Ariel confirmed my inner knowing that ending my marriage was the right decision, even in the face of strong adversity. I was being protected by the angelic realms and this gave me courage to continue the path. Archangel Ariel also offered that through my conviction and execution of this life-changing decision, I may one day become a role model for others. Perhaps one day I could give someone else the strength to stand up for themselves, for their own life, for their own future—for the highest good of all involved.

I drew real strength from this reading and began to believe that perhaps I wasn't alone, and the universe really was loving, guiding and supporting me. It reminded me of the archetype of the Scorpio—death and rebirth. Perhaps it was time for my true Scorpio nature to unfold. The death, though, had to come first.

So began the most heart-wrenching and incredibly sad part of my journey up to this point. I had to face the death of my marriage. I had to summon all my courage and have the conversation with my husband. It was time to let him know our 14-year relationship had come to an end.

After dinner one evening, having just put the girls to bed, I uttered the fateful words "we need to talk". My stomach was in knots and I could barely breathe. I was not just anxious, I was terrified.

We sat together at our dining room table. I knew I would not remember everything I wanted or needed to say so I opened my notepad where I had prepared a list of points to discuss. I delivered my carefully prepared speech, watching his reaction to my words. I waited patiently for his response.

He had always been a balanced and considered man, and even in the most traumatic and challenging of situations he managed to retain a sense of calm, a sense of self.

After a prolonged silence, the discussion began. We talked for about an hour that evening. Not once did he ask why I was ending our marriage. He just accepted my decision. He didn't fight for me. He didn't fight for us. Perhaps it was already over for him too? Or perhaps he knew me better than I knew myself. Perhaps he knew that to fight for someone who was already lost was not going to yield a different outcome.

That night, as I retreated to the master bedroom alone for the first time in 14 years, I asked for only one message. It was Archangel Azrael who came to me:

COMFORT – ARCHANGEL AZRAEL
"I am with you in your time of need, helping your heart to heal."

Say. No. More.

The afternoon we arrived home from Bali, I received another astonishingly accurate, timely message from my angelic team. It was after I read Jason's short and dismissive email, the one where he said no.

After the unpacking was complete, the washing on and the girls asleep, I settled into bed and consulted my archangel deck. Real life was beginning again. I had to focus all my attention on my new reality and begin the process of moving forward and rebuilding my life without my soulmate by my side, or even in my life. I asked the question: *In my highest good and for the highest good of all, what are the key messages I need to receive now?*

Archangel Raziel, Archangel Raguel and Archangel Uriel came to me that evening.

TAKE BACK YOUR POWER – ARCHANGEL RAZIEL
"Use your God-given power and intention to manifest blessings in your life."

RELATIONSHIP HARMONY – ARCHANGEL RAGUEL
"We angels are opening the hearts of everyone involved. Arguments and conflicts are being resolved now."

YOU KNOW WHAT TO DO – ARCHANGEL URIEL
"Trust your inner knowledge, and act upon it without delay."

Clear, focused, targeted messages from the angelic realms. It was time to take back my power and trust in my developing spiritual strength. It was time to lovingly and firmly move forward and draw upon the resources of Spirit to guide my way. I was reminded to act from a place of heart-centred consciousness in recognition that change is uncomfortable—and devastating for my children, husband, family and friends—but in truth, change was required.

It was critical to remember my children and husband were blessings in my life and to keep this awareness front of mind as I navigated the destabilising, even tumultuous time that lay ahead.

I also needed to be receptive to the idea that Jason was a blessing, and that love was at the centre of our incredibly brief encounter. Perhaps he was sent to me by the universe, by my angels, so I would make the necessary changes for the highest good of all involved? And although my heart broke every time I considered my future without him, it was time to redirect my energy back to me.

Turns out, the universe had been providing guidance relating to my future with Jason all along. It was just my stubbornness, sadness and incredulity (come on, he was there too!) that had not been willing—perhaps not been able—to assimilate it. I believe Spirit only gives you the messages you are capable of hearing at any given point in time. That also includes your interpretation of the messages.

A few months after I met Jason, I was still in the land of heartache and despair for the level of trauma I had caused those I dearly loved. Nevertheless, I was full of optimism and hope for a future with Jason even though he had decided not to take the leap with me. Sure, we hadn't fallen immediately into each other's arms, but I still couldn't see my future through any other lens than happily ever after with my soulmate. I was in a holding pattern, waiting patiently for him to recognise the depth of connection we shared.

I was now using a new oracle deck recommended to me called Wisdom of the Oracle by Colette Baron-Reid. This deck is a firm favourite and the only deck outside of Archangel Oracle I relied on in those first few months.

I asked the question: *In my highest good, and in the highest good for us both, what would be the result of entering into a relationship with Jason?*

The cards drawn from this new deck were:

WHY?

Essential meanings: *Motives driving intention; the power of knowing the 'why'.*

I certainly wasn't thrilled with this first message, drawn in protection mode. It inferred I was subconsciously denying the truth as it didn't align with my desire. Indeed it didn't—my heart, my soul and my ego could only see my future with Jason.

I knew the phrase from the booklet *"you believe that your love continues to be strong, but deep down what you really desire is to have the last word with that person"* didn't fit me entirely. I just wanted to have any words exchanged with Jason. I was desperate to understand how he was feeling and, crucially, if our meeting meant anything to him. The message also asked me to search for the 'why' but that was all I had been doing for months! It was a soul-crushing card to be offered!

SERENDIPITY

Essential meanings: *Opportunity allied with readiness; the awareness of synchronicity; luck and good fortune appearing as signs and symbols; a magical alignment of events.*

I was not too thrilled about this second card in protection either. I did believe our serendipitous meeting was *"meant to lead to something better"* and the *"person I gave my heart to was supposed to be 'the one'"*. Absolutely, why else would we have met? Of course it was meant to end in happily ever after!

Did I consider for a second that *"synchronicity and serendipity came together to lead you* (me) *directly into difficulties to deliver an important lesson you (I) need to learn* before *you (I) hit the jackpot"?* No, I had tunnel vision and could only see life the way I wanted it to unfold. No lessons required, no other jackpot necessary. I was more than satisfied with the jackpot I had already won.

The only silver lining I could see through the trauma and upheaval I was creating was the certain fact my happily ever after with Jason was only delayed. It clearly wasn't quite the right time for our union. It was, in my mind, still an absolute. Another ridiculous card, thanks so much!

BLESSED

Essential meanings: *Something wonderful that is unearned and unexpected; grace that is an unforeseen gift from Spirit.*

The whole message of Blessed in protection resonated with me. Jason was clearly a gift from the universe as I was on the wrong path and needed a course correction. *"In a way you have hit rock bottom, and what is required now is nothing less than total surrender."* Well, let's just say if this was my rock bottom the book would end here, but I wasn't even close to rock bottom; this was just round one.

As I wrote this section, I chose a card from Colette Baron-Reid's Goddess Power Oracle (another firm favourite—thank you, Colette!) and I asked: *On this day, as I sit down to write this book, which Goddess is with me?*

SARASWATI – GODDESS OF MASTERY

It's card 44. I am 44 years of age.

Saraswati spoke directly to my situation—inviting me to dedicate a period of time and commit to entering into the Goddess's domain of language, art and poetry with all my senses. Her message was that if I learn a craft and dedicate myself to continuous learning, I will eventually become a true master.

Ummm, okay. Again, wow.

I didn't sit down to write this book as a professional writer; I'm just a woman who feels called to tell her story with the hope and belief that it will benefit other souls on their own unique journey. I am an eager apprentice, willing to devote my time and effort, with my heart and with my soul, to learn the creative art of writing.

I approach these times with my little book as a joyful experience. It's never a chore, never something on the to-do list, never a burden and never with any expectation. If I write a sentence or a chapter, it doesn't matter. If I have a wonderful 'fill up my cup' day of writing then don't sit down again for weeks, it doesn't matter. What matters is when I speak, I do so from the heart with the intention of being of service.

❖

Whilst researching the history of divination and oracle cards, I sought guidance from both Doreen Virtue and Colette Baron-Reid's websites. Whilst Colette's website was rich with information and guidance, wholeheartedly endorsing the divination properties of oracle cards, Doreen Virtue converted to Christianity in 2017 and no longer sells or condones her New Age oracle decks. I respect her and her decision. My experience with these cards has shifted my life in profound and wonderful ways, and even though her journey has taken her on a different path, I am deeply grateful for her contribution to the world of oracle cards. I couldn't imagine my life without them!

Signs From the Universe

"The universe works in mysterious ways." I had heard this expression many times but had never given it too much consideration. After all, I wasn't plugged in to the universe or its abundance until my awakening began. Maybe in small amounts—a fortuitous conversation with someone that nudged me forward, or a coincidental event that made me wonder just how coincidental it was—but I certainly didn't understand the depth and breadth of abundance on offer.

The universe is constantly working to make available the people, resources, situations and lessons required for us to become the people we are *meant* to become. Once I started paying attention, I realised I was being shown where I needed to go and what I needed to do to create the life of my dreams. When I wasn't listening, the universe found a way (usually dramatically or traumatically!) to command my attention. I was shown in no uncertain terms that I needed to course correct, and quickly.

For all those times I felt I couldn't go on—when I would fall into depression and despair—the universe always managed to find a way to communicate with me in such a way that I found the strength and the courage to just keep going.

Over time, with practice and patience, I have relaxed into the experience of listening to the universe and decoding its messages. But it wasn't easy, and it didn't happen overnight. Often I was just too busy to spend a microsecond thinking if a message was meant for me. I then went through a stage where EVERYTHING I saw, felt and heard was for me. Now I check in with my intuition to see if the message resonates, or if I let it pass through my consciousness and straight out the other side.

"JASON"

I'll start with the obvious: the name Jason. (Remember, names have been changed to protect identities!)

Let's just say in the months after meeting "Jason" I saw and heard the name everywhere! Jason is the name of my favourite action actor. I'd discover a catchy new song on Spotify only to look at my phone and see the artist's name was Jason. I'd meet a lovely car repair man who went out of his way to help a damsel in distress, whose name was—you guessed it—Jason. I'd meet an interesting new client and, of course, his name was Jason. The examples go on and on.

Obvious call-out here—Jason is not an uncommon name. It is a biblical name: it is a saint's name in both the Catholic and Greek Orthodox religions. Its popularity has never waned, so if I wanted to find multiple references to Jason, to validate this section of the book, it could easily be done!

At first, every time I saw the name Jason it was confirmation that our reunion was imminent. It was absolute. In those first few months the universe knew the only way I was going to survive the experience of meeting my soulmate was to interpret the seeing or hearing of the name as evidence that my future was with him, living happily ever after.

I now understand it was the universe's way of loving and protecting me from the truth. It would have been too much to cope with, the devastation too overwhelming, had my consciousness clocked that my future did not include him.

On my walk to the ferry each day the first street I must cross is Jason Street. It's the very first street sign I see upon leaving the sanctuary of my apartment. For many months I would oscillate between joy and despair, heartache and hope. It was a reminder, twice a day, of how much my life had changed.

On good days, when I was in the zone and believed our reconciliation was imminent, I would look up at the sign, smile and say, "Good morning" (yes, out loud). I would fantasise this was, of course, a clear sign he would make his way back to me and we would make our way into the future together.

On other days when my faith wavered, I would struggle not to fall into despair, and it would take every ounce of my willpower to continue into the city. The rollercoaster of emotions was intense and completely depleting.

Despite the remarkable forward progress I had made in most areas of my life, I never really believed it would not, eventually, be him. I was in a holding pattern, patiently waiting for him to recognise the gravity of the connection we shared. Waiting for him to acknowledge that our soul connection was way too precious, was indeed incredibly rare (the phrase 'one in a million' comes to mind), and a once-in-a-lifetime gift.

Then one morning I was standing at my kitchen window, and although my dialogue with the universe was strong and clear, the question once again resurfaced—how could our connection not lead to happily ever after? (Again, I am a very slow learner and incredibly stubborn.) I said out loud, "Okay, give me another sign it really isn't him."

I finished dressing for work and marched down to the ferry towards the street sign. I burst out laughing, right there, in the middle of the footpath. It was just past 7:00 a.m. and there were two council workmen taking down the street sign. Literally taking it DOWN! Right in front of me. Not five minutes after my request for yet another sign that it wasn't him. I shook my head in disbelief. And thankfully, it happened at a time I could laugh along with it. Spirit certainly has a sense of humour!

On a daily basis, and in all manner of places, the name Jason continues to appear. It's the way I interpret these signs now that has fundamentally changed—if I take them as signs at all.

I will be forever thankful he came into my life. His impact has been remarkable, his legacy life changing. He led me back to myself. For that gift I will forever be in gratitude to his soul.

SPIRIT OVER THE AIRWAVES

Mercifully my signs haven't all been about Jason. As my journey continued, I began to open up to messages relating to other parts of my life. Here's an entry from my diary, a few weeks after meeting Jason:

I enjoyed my infrared sauna tonight and listened to my favourite talkback radio show. I find the messages are somehow tailored for me, even though the host may be dispersing advice for another soul on the other side of the world. Somehow, I feel the messages are for me as well as for the caller.

The advice for a caller who was having to start again from scratch was to start a playlist of music for her future life. The song suggested, out of the millions and millions and millions of songs in the universe, was 'I'm Coming Out' by Diana Ross. There are no words. My angels are extremely strong, and I am listening and hearing them more and more, stronger and stronger their voices.

They give me continued faith in my journey and ensure that if I feel a little nervous or scared or doubtful, they guide me back to the decision I have made to leave my marriage and that it's the right decision for all involved.

Another night in my sauna, in the very early days of my awakening, I had the following thought. I wrote the details in my diary that evening:

A long-lost memory resurfaced in my conscious tonight (again, it's the angels sending these memories to me) that I had once been told by a clairvoyant my children would come through me quickly and at the time they were meant to, as I had other things that needed doing in my life. And my husband was deliberately chosen to be their father as he'd be a lifelong devoted constant to them.

That I would be 'busy' and not as available to them on my next life path. And the interest and joy I experience with my recent 'angel awakening' makes me wonder if my spiritual side may take more precedence in my life in my future ... maybe that's my new journey?

And then I had a strange premonition of being interviewed about a book and I recounted the story of meeting my guardian angel in the form of a tall, dark and handsome man who within a few hours changed my life ... if this turns out to be true.

This has all come true.

The advice to find the song 'I'm Coming Out' by Diana Ross was a mere two weeks after my walk along the beach where it magically entered my earphones and became the first song on my first playlist.

My children arrived quickly and easily. I was incredibly blessed to have no conception problems, falling pregnant exactly when I planned to. Given I was 34 years old, was stressed to my eyeballs from my demanding corporate job in investment banking at the height of the global financial crisis and was carrying a significant amount of extra weight, it was indeed a miracle.

I chose the father of my children exceptionally well—he is an outstanding, dedicated father to my two precious girls.

Then of course Mr. Tall, Dark and Handsome appeared in my life at a most unexpected time, under the most exceptional circumstances, and fundamentally altered my life's direction.

And the book? Well, if you are reading this, that part has also come true.

SONGS SEND THE MESSAGE

Eighteen months after meeting Jason, my focus had been firmly redirected to my ongoing healing and towards the next chapter of my life. I was owning my decisions and my future happiness, and although my life's path wasn't fully illuminated, confidence and belief in my ability to win at this game of life was strong.

From my journal:

I am in the Sydney CBD at 8:00 a.m. hanging out in this cool office building that has a very on-trend breakout area and a coffee shop—perfect for my requisite morning coffee. I put my headphones on and choose a random Spotify playlist, just for fun. "What's the message for me today, universe?" I ask confidently, knowing full well I will be sent exactly what I need to hear.

The song 'Higher Love' by Kygo and Whitney Houston begins to play. Immediately the universe validates me—I am on the right track. I am open to higher love as I now know higher love exists. Spiritual love exists. Spiritual connections exist. I am secure in myself and willing to wait. The right man will find me at the exact right time for my soul's evolution, and I will arrive at the exact right time for him. We will then make the journey forward together.

I have surrendered. I trust. I am more 'me' than I have been for many years. I am now 'plugged in' to the universe. I am happy.

ANGEL NUMBERS

As I write this chapter sitting on my couch, I look out the window of my apartment to the house across the street. I have seen this house hundreds of times. The house number is on the front gate where it's always been, and I have observed it many times. It is house number 11. Then I look to the right, again certainly not for the first time, where number 11 is on the front door to the house. From a distance they are visually side by side—1111. 1111 is an angel number. It's been there all along, but as I picked up my laptop today and glanced out of the window, preparing myself to start this chapter, I see it. I really *see* the sign for the first time.

The sign was delivered to me just as I was beginning to sink into the fear that this book won't help anyone; indeed, that no one will actually be interested in reading it! That the only purpose of this tap-tap-tapping away is to delay the realisation that the life I am leading is out of alignment and I crave change. I yearn for a life more interesting, exciting and certainly less stressful. A life that doesn't just feel like work.

Perhaps it's just a ridiculous, delusional, self-serving fantasy and my friends are just smirking and laughing behind my back? As if my life could possibly be interesting enough to read about!

No. I stop my thoughts right there. I am meant to write this book. It is meant to be in the world. My life is meant to serve as a tangible expression of what the universe we live in is capable of delivering if you trust, surrender and believe. I now always seek the lesson I am being taught. Upon uncovering and integrating the lesson, the pain becomes lighter. Emotion is of course energy in motion. Now I am able to recognise it and let it move through me so as not to allow an ache to linger in my body, heart or soul.

You are being supported, and you need to know it. Life has meaning, it has purpose—it can deliver incredible soulful growth if you are willing to go deep and do the work. Your life has the capacity to be not only joyful and full of love, but of service to many people in multitudes of ways.

I pour myself a cup of herbal tea, pick up my laptop and continue to write. I am worthy of love and I am being cared for by a kind and benevolent universe. I continue in faith and trust and will see this book through to its conclusion, whenever that may be.

Elevating and Emerging

It had been ten months since meeting Jason and for all intents and purposes I appeared to have adjusted remarkably well. The family home had been sold. I had moved to a fabulous apartment with spectacular views through Sydney Heads. The girls had adjusted admirably to their changed home circumstances. My ex-husband and I were enjoying an amicable relationship. My professional life was back on track after those incredibly difficult first few months. And the changes to my diet and exercise were yielding impressive results.

It wasn't, though, entirely true. There was one part of my life I hadn't been able to heal. I couldn't stop thinking of Jason. I hadn't dismissed the idea of a life together. I hadn't been able to let him go. In my mind, heart and soul I still couldn't envisage a future without him by my side, living happily ever after.

You may be shaking your head at me by now, rolling your eyes or even yelling at this page, and I don't blame you at all.

The logical part of my brain is 100 percent with you. It was screaming at me: "He said NO, Amanda. TWICE!!! Enough already. Move on. You have made such remarkable changes for the better yet you still dwell in the energy of a man you spent such a short amount of time with. You are delusional. Just get over it!"

I couldn't though, I couldn't just get over it. I had been broken apart, yet I had never felt so complete, so safe, so connected. I had never known love like that before.

I made the incredibly brave decision (see also: embarrassing, foolish, ridiculous) to reach out to him one last time. I needed to know, once and for all (again!) if my future might still be with him or if I had to truly make my way forward by myself. Again, just remarkably stubborn!

I had of course wanted to reach out many times over the past months but in my heart, I knew I wasn't ready. I was too raw, the connection too real, the consequences too devastating if he had moved on without a thought of me. It took me ten months before I could reach out again. It took me ten months as I intuitively understood I had to be strong enough in myself to survive if his answer was (still) no.

My journal writings that day:

I am doing my best to remain positive of our connection and the opportunity for us to reconnect. To come together and thrive. It is taking so much strength to remain in this energy as with each day that goes by it becomes harder to keep the faith. Any logical person not tuned into their energy would think I was foolish and delirious. Am I? Am I crazy???

I want to believe my spiritual team is guiding me, loving and supporting me. My faith keeps me optimistic about the future. If I didn't have this strength and conviction this soulmate connection was real, I'm not sure how I'd be coping. I need to trust. I need to trust divine guidance and divine timing.

Whilst sitting at Melbourne airport after an exhausting business trip I asked my angels via my Wisdom of the Oracle deck for guidance. I asked for only one piece of advice: *In my highest good and in the highest good for all, what is your guidance regarding reaching out to Jason?*

COME TO THE EDGE

Essential meanings: *Courage, taking a leap of faith, overcoming fear and accepting risk.*

The answer was clear! There are 52 cards in the deck, and I asked for only one. One piece of guidance to confirm if I should reach out to Jason or let the connection rest. It was clearly time to come to the edge, have courage, take a leap of faith, overcome my fear and take the risk in communication.

My only choice was to express my true feelings, my true self. I had to be open and vulnerable and let Jason into the secret I had been hiding so well. I hadn't let him go, I was in love with him—or perhaps I was in love with what his soul had awakened within me?

I had written the letter in my journal many times over the past few months. I typed it again that day as I waited in the airport lounge. With my guidance received, butterflies in my stomach and nervous energy tingling throughout my body, I pressed send. I took my seat in the plane, turned my phone off and flew home to Sydney. There was now no turning back (or retracting the message, if that ever works anyway?). For the next hour I daydreamed of my future—with Jason of course. But it was about to become real.

Hi Jason
I hope this email finds you well. I wanted to reach out and check in, as I find myself thinking of you and continue to feel a huge amount of appreciation for our brief time together last year.
I am so much happier than I was when we met. I just didn't

realise with how busy life is, how much I needed my life to change. The separation was fairly fuss and pain free—and overdue. The girls have been coping really well, and I'm sure that's as a result of the amicable way we both approached the split.

I'm living in a fabulous apartment, having sold the family home. The girls are with me week on week off, and love living near the beach and wandering down the hill for dinner whenever we like.

Work has been busy, as usual, but I seem to be coping better than I was. It's not where I see myself forever, but it's allowing me to progress and build so I can (hopefully) cut down on both time and energy commitments in the near future ...

I don't know if I've even entered your consciousness since last year, but I feel compelled to reconnect and just ask you. I'd call, but I could only find your work phone and it's probably not an office conversation!

Anyway, it would be lovely to hear from you. I hope you're doing well.

Amanda

As I landed in Sydney, knots invaded my stomach and I struggled to breathe. I turned on my phone and checked my emails. There was a message. The message that would direct and perhaps even alter the course of my life. To my utter astonishment I couldn't immediately read it.

I made my way to the train, then to the ferry. It was a glorious evening where the harbour glistened in the setting sun. Water has always had a soothing effect on me, and I briefly relaxed and enjoyed the journey. Then it hit me. The email was waiting. It was time to know.

I opened my phone and read the message. I read it once. I read it twice. I put the phone away as the ferry docked.

The answer was no. Again. He had moved on, was living with someone, and was happy. He had thought about me but didn't divulge the extent of this, nor his feelings (if any) for me.

Again, I couldn't breathe. My body was physically weak, my emotional energy was completely depleted, and I was so disoriented that, for a moment, I couldn't even remember if I needed to turn left or right when disembarking from the ferry. I felt like I had been hit by a truck from the outside and the inside.

I made my way home in a daze and went straight to bed. I was hosting my cousin Erin and her friend Sharon for the weekend (to go bridesmaid dress shopping for Erin's upcoming Hawaiian wedding, no less), so I numbed myself with copious amounts of wine to prolong the need to feel my feelings. I now knew, with certainty, my future did not involve Jason.

It's okay if you thought you were over it, but it hits you all over again. It's okay to fall apart even after you thought you had it under control. You are not weak. Healing is messy. There is no timeline for healing
Diana Zamora

I survived the next month and I don't use the word 'survived' lightly.

As Easter approached it dawned on me that I had a four-day holiday with only myself for company as the children would be with their father. I didn't relish being alone whilst friends busied themselves with their families, so I booked into a health and wellness resort in the rolling vineyards of the Hunter Valley called Elysia Wellness Retreat. Those four days, at considerable expense, saved my life.

During the retreat I enjoyed long walks through the rugged Australian countryside, practised various forms of yoga, participated in full body stretching sessions, blissed out in guided meditations with music soothing my soul, flexed my muscles in 'balance ball' classes and slept. I did a lot of sleeping. I was energetically depleted so I would skip the active afternoon gym classes and instead treat myself to massages and facials and water therapy treatments.

The balance of light physical activity, relaxing meditations, indulgent therapies and nutritious cuisine resourced me enough to just keep going. Again, I don't write this lightly; I mean every word. There have been so many times I didn't think I would make it, that I would survive this experience. How grateful I am now that I did.

A critical piece of my healing puzzle was a session with the in-house spiritual healer. It was one and a half hours of (mainly me) talking. I explained the reason for booking the appointment—the story of meeting Jason and the decisions I subsequently made, his decision to leave me in his past and the single life I was now living. She penned a mantra for me whilst I shared my story. She drew an elaborate graphic around the mantra and the words sprang to life:

I am here, as I am arriving
I am known, as I am knowing
I am understanding the truth of who I am
I am emerging
I am meeting and I am merging with this ocean of oneness within
I am the love I have been seeking
I am home.

I was asked to recite the mantra out loud seven times, but I was crying so hard I couldn't even speak it once. I sat in the chair, wholly unrecognisable to myself. I tried to recite the mantra multiple times. Then it happened. I felt my heart break.

As we wrapped up our session, tears still streaming down my face, she revealed her thoughts to me. She didn't believe I had met my soulmate in Margaret River. She believed I reunited, in this lifetime, with my twin flame.

❖

The recitation of my mantra was tough, but I did it. I persisted. Seven times in the morning and seven times at night. I was instructed to complete this exercise for 14 days, but my intuition told me that until I could recite it out loud without crying, and manage to do so over several consecutive days, I wasn't ready to move forward.

It took me 21 days. At day 21, I felt calm, clear, at peace. I had finally assimilated the message into the depths of my soul. I even smiled to myself. Ten months after meeting my soulmate, I had done it. I had found the love I had been seeking externally; I had found it within.

I enjoyed two more visits to Elysia Retreat with girlfriends the following year which were much less agonising, much more relaxed and definitely more pleasurable. It became a retreat filled with laughter and luxurious day spa treatments with some physical exertion thrown in for good measure. Ten-kilometre mountainous hike, anyone? Bring it on!

I returned home with an increased sense of confidence in my physical abilities, my emotional world, my connection with the universe and with myself. I was developing the internal confidence not only to handle life, but to thrive in the new life I was creating.

Soul Retrieval

Travel has always been an integral part of my life. My parents owned travel agencies when I was young so when everyone went to the beach for summer, I went to Europe to snow ski. Quite the trip from Australia! It was a fabulous perk of the travel industry and my family took full advantage of it. Travel has continued to be an important part of my life, of my identity. I might not escape to Europe or Canada to ski every year—as I am now paying for it myself!— but I enjoy extensive travel throughout Asia and the occasional American and European adventure.

About 18 months after meeting Jason I challenged myself and embarked on my first solo overseas journey. Well, almost solo; I sort of cheated. I joined a group tour company called Flash Pack for solo travellers in their 30s and 40s that happened to appear in my Facebook feed one day (those algorithms!). What an amazing company.

I chose Argentina for my solo adventure as I had never explored South America and an itinerary that included a street art tour of Buenos Aires, hiking the Perito Moreno Glacier in Patagonia, and riding a bike through the Mendoza wine region sampling malbec and pinot noir ticked all my adventure and palate boxes.

There were, however, fears I had to overcome. Who was I without my (ex)husband and children standing beside me? Who was I without my corporate uniform on? Without my business card identifying me as someone who had a successful career and was worthy of engagement? Who was I without close friends ready with reliable conversation and giggles? Without my history well known, without the comfort of familiar faces? What would happen if I was just Amanda?

It was time to find out. I booked the tour, boarded the plane, took (many) deep breaths and embarked on my South American adventure.

Catch me in the right energy and I'm social and gregarious. I am articulate and can be quite amusing, particularly in a self-deprecating way. I can hold a conversation and have an opinion on most things— not always well informed or researched, but that never stops me sharing! I developed and honed many extrovert personality traits early on in life and have gravitated to career roles that required these skills.

But in truth, and as I mature, I recognise it's an act. Perhaps a coping mechanism in itself. I can hide from my true self by being an exaggerated form of self. I am actually an introvert. I have spent time reflecting on this categorisation of my personality and I now recognise this truth. So, with personal acceptance of my more reserved nature, I embarked on this adventure in alignment with my true self. It took courage to remove the extroverted mask I had been wearing my whole life. I felt raw. I felt exposed. But I did it.

Argentina turned out to be far more beneficial on the mind, the body and the soul than I could have possibly imagined or dared hope for. I spent the first few days by myself exploring the incredibly diverse city of Buenos Aires. I strolled through Plaza de Mayo steeped rich in history, visited La Boca football stadium, wandered the streets of The Caminito with its brightly coloured terrace houses with sculptures of famous Argentines waving from the balconies, and took a tour of the Teatro Colon Opera House modelled on the best European architecture.

I spent another day getting lost in the laneways of the San Telmo market that serves some of the best empanadas in the country, wandered Recoleta Cemetery where your status (and wealth) from life transferred to death, and ended the day in the hip area of Palermo with its eclectic dining experiences and boutique bars dressed up as ageing apocatheries. My palate was well entertained, and I quickly learnt to eat a light breakfast and lunch, saving myself for the mouth-watering steaks accompanied by delicious malbec for dinner!

When the Flash Pack tour began I set off, determinedly, as the real Amanda. And it was fabulous! I met wonderful people, enjoyed incredible experiences and formed a few friendships that continue to this day. Acutely aware of the promise I made to myself, I did not set false expectations of who I was. Case in point, I'm just not a night-time party girl. I enjoy being home and tucked up in bed by 10:00 p.m.

After dinner I'd thank everyone for a great evening and waddle, full of steak and wine, back to the hotel. I wasn't going to pretend to be someone I'm not just to fit in, nor did I have the stamina to drink all night with the younger party crowd. And you know what? It was okay! Sure, it meant that I wasn't privy to all the gossip and shenanigans that occurred in the wee hours of the morning, but I made peace with that. I was becoming more confident in who I was, and my self-esteem strengthened as I respected and honoured myself.

I pushed myself physically too on this Argentinian adventure. One of the activities was an all-day hike to the top of Mount Fitz Roy in

El Chalten, deep in the Patagonian landscape. We woke to a glorious, clear and warmish day where the weather board boasted of perfect hiking conditions. I hadn't been well but took the appropriate medications and set off to scale a mountain I would never have considered attempting on my own. It was a challenge I didn't know I could conquer.

The lead group of eight made it to the peak after four hours, which was an incredible achievement. However, just as we reached the peak the weather deteriorated quickly. The glorious sunny day gave way to punishing rain and winds gusting over 40 km per hour. The power of the wind was almost enough to blow us clear off the hiking track. But there was nothing we could do except keep moving. No one was going to come and save us; we had to save ourselves. At an elevation of 3,000 metres and 30,000 steps.

Upon returning to base camp I was completely soaked through but exhilarated and immensely proud of myself. And I certainly wasn't the slowest of our group, easily eclipsing some of the younger hikers which surprised and, to be honest, impressed the hell out of me! I glanced at the signboard as we left the park. The display had been changed from perfect conditions to extreme conditions— DO NOT HIKE!

I was also becoming confident in the universe's ability to communicate with me and received many signs clearly meant for me whilst on my trip.

One evening we were dining in a restaurant in El Calafate with breathtaking views of the setting sun over Lago del Desierto. As we left the restaurant a gorgeous dog appeared in the foyer. It was a cross between a golden retriever and a cocker spaniel. It had beautiful caramel-brown fur and a happy, engaging disposition. We couldn't help ourselves from fawning over this wonderful animal. Then out of the blue, one of the girls named the dog. She named it Jason. Seriously?!?!? And then she laughed and offered that she'd never actually heard of a dog called Jason before ... and continued to chuckle.

Of course, I had to reflect that evening as I went to bed. Is it meant to be a reference to Jason, or is there another man named Jason that I am going to meet? Or does the name Jason now represent something bigger for me?

Was my lighter response to this evidence of how much healing I had accomplished? Had I really progressed as much as I gave myself credit for? Was the universe being cheeky and testing my acceptance of life without Jason by my side? As I snuggled under the blankets in my beautifully appointed hotel room that evening I received a clear message from the angelic realms: *Spirit is with me, I'm on the right track with my life, I am always protected and always guided wherever I may be in the world.* I looked towards the heavens, smiled, and said, "Thank you," before falling into a blissful slumber.

Another highlight was the spiritual growth and deepening connection to my soul I experienced.

Argentina had never featured on my travel bucket list (and it was an extensive list) but I knew there was a reason I boarded the plane to South America and not Europe or Asia for this holiday. I discussed my choice of destination with my transference healing practitioner (more on this modality later), posing the question to her. "Perhaps you'll know when you get there," was her answer. I just sat with her response and was consciously open to what the universe had, if anything, to offer. Turns out, it did.

I was awake early one morning in El Chalten, so decided to set out from our rustic cattle ranch for a meander through the long grasses and indigenous trees. I wasn't going anywhere in particular but felt the desire to just be in the awe-inspiring, expansive landscape.

I walked a kilometre or two towards the glistening lake where iceberg tips bobbled about and then just ... stopped. I looked around and I felt it. The knowledge and the 'knowing' were immediate. I had been here before. It wasn't in this lifetime, but I had lived a prior life amongst the people of Patagonia. I knew it as sure as I knew the sky was blue. It struck me immediately in my soul, and it took my breath away. I had come home.

I was in the part of the country aligned with the root chakra of the body. The root chakra is located at the base of the spine and provides the foundation upon which we build our life. It is where we ground ourselves into the earth and anchor our energy in the world. If our root chakra is out of balance we may find it hard to feel safe, perceiving the world to be full of risks, which then leads to living life from a place of fear instead of trust.

As I stood in absolute stillness, deep in the heart of Patagonia, my decision to explore Argentina immediately made absolutely perfect sense. I wrote with elation in my diary that morning:

I now know why I am here—I have come to Argentina to ground. To heal my root chakra. To repair the foundation of my life, to move forward, fully supported. It's very moving. I am in tears as I write this, driving through the most magnificent, awe-inspiring scenery.

I am healing my root chakra and reading about it at the same time in Anatomy of the Spirit by Caroline Myss. I am healing and growing, and it is overwhelming.

I have cried a few times on this trip. For different reasons. Sometimes a little unsure of what I am doing here. Sometimes a little worried about how I will be in a group dynamic. Sometimes a little worried about my future when I temporarily forget the universe is taking care of me and I am exactly where I need to be right now.

I am in Patagonia and I am retrieving a lost part of my soul.

I experienced a fundamental shift that day and it has propelled me forward—into my life, into my body, into my soul and back into the world in which I now live. I will be forever grateful for my Argentine adventure.

Within a month of returning home I had booked my next adventure with Flash Pack. I was hooked!

This time my destination of choice was Morocco. Again, I didn't know why I had chosen where or when I was going, but I was confident that by the time I had experienced my Moroccan adventure I would know exactly why.

The gift of time since Argentina has confirmed that being authentically Amanda—just as I am—is more than enough. I wasn't the out-all-night party girl, yet I was liked and accepted. I didn't require my business card, husband or children to prove my worth. My travelling companions sought me out to spend time with me. They enjoyed my company and wanted to get to know me on a deeper level. On reflection, this trip was crucial for rebuilding my self-confidence that had been decimated not only by Jason's rejection but the friendships that had dissolved since Margaret River.

4.
The Changing Landscape of Friendships

I am understanding the truth of who I am

I am emerging ...

It's one of the awakening journey's most cruel surprises. Just when you need your friends the most, some will disappear.

After dedicated time in quiet contemplation, I realised it's actually been happening my whole life. The invitations for a meal or drink together dried up, even though there was a time we would spend every waking second joined at the hip. There comes a time where one person stops calling or texting back.

When I initially told a few close friends about meeting Jason the reactions were varied, as expected. Some worried I was making a life-changing mistake by leaving a very good man to walk into the unknown, some were completely supportive and recognised my foundation had been shaken in such a profound way that I didn't have a choice and some didn't even bother to ask. Indeed, to this day, some of my closest friends don't actually know why I made the decision to leave my husband.

This has been a very difficult reality of this journey and has fundamentally altered my relationships with some souls forever.

Strengthening

My friends who listened to the story of Jason understood my life had irrevocably changed. They may have thought I was crazy, irrational or just going through a stage (not completely foreign as I do have a flare for the dramatic at times), but most were supportive, accepting and stood by my decision.

An incredible gift of this journey has been the development of genuine, deep, truthful connections on a level I never considered possible. An experience like this mandates authenticity and vulnerability to survive. One simply can't bottle up all emotions and move through it alone. Well, some might manage it, but I couldn't.

There are four women I want to extend a big, warm, embracing, universal hug to. These women were fundamental to my survival in those early days and became my core cheerleading squad as I found my way back to me. They were there at the bottom of the harbour dragging me from the depths and swimming me back to shore. Their support, time, energy, forbearance and willingness to travel with me in non-judgement is a gift that can never be truly repaid.

I have come to recognise these friends as soulmates too. Not the romantic kind, but soulmates in the sense that we are in this particular adventure on earth together at this time. I hold these precious souls dear to me and am incredibly grateful for their presence in my life. For as long as our connection lasts, I will love and cherish them. I will love and support them. I will love and delight in them.

My heart belongs to Charmayne in particular, as she has been unfailingly generous with her time, understanding and unconditional love. Her unwavering support has been a crucial source of strength and comfort.

When I returned from Margaret River I was desperate to relay the incredible experience of meeting Jason, so she promptly rearranged her schedule to accommodate a bushwalk and coffee. I could barely contain my excitement! She patiently indulged my re-enactment of every scene, look, touch and kiss I experienced. I don't think I drew breath for an hour. She was speechless.

She was my main partner in all the lunches and dinners (and bottles of wine), exhibiting a generous amount of tolerance for the rehashing of my stories and indulging my aspirations for the future.

Throughout my journey she delicately delivered advice in the spirit of love in such a way for me to hear it without taking offence. I would not always receive it immediately but she would patiently wait for me to integrate and assimilate her counsel. I would get there, most times, in the end.

Crucially, she cradled my heart when it became clear Jason and I would not share a future, constantly affirming I was becoming stronger and more capable in myself—by myself—every day. She was there for me on the days—so many days—I didn't believe I would make it through.

Everyone needs a Charmayne: a person who will celebrate the triumphs, indulge in even the most outlandish fantasies (to a point), and lift you out of despair when all hope has left your body. My heart swells with the deepest of emotion every time I think of her. I am so incredibly blessed to have her in my life.

Tess and I were brought together by our daughters at daycare and have become good friends over the years. She and Steve were one of the couples we travelled to Bali with, and they were very supportive of both my ex-husband and I during that very difficult holiday. Even though her life was incredibly busy, she spent hours listening patiently to my struggles over bottles of rosé at her kitchen table.

She extended invitations for pizza on Friday nights when it was clear I wasn't coping with life as a single mother. She ferried my daughter to and from sports activities so I could focus on work and keep one part of my life on track (crucial when you only have yourself to rely on). She also spent the first New Year's Eve after the separation with me as she recognised I just wasn't strong enough to attend our mutual friend's party.

Just thinking about the tenderness and generosity she extended to me during that time has the power to reduce me to grateful tears.

Krystyna has been a close friend of mine for many years and we remain an integral part of each other's lives to this day. We enjoy nothing more than catching up over a few glasses of wine at her kitchen bench or sitting on her verandah sipping cups of herbal tea— depending on the time of the day and our mood at the time!

Our conversations are as diverse as they could possibly be. We can begin in the world of financial services and corporate life, segue easily into entrepreneurial ventures, then pivot effortlessly to spirituality. Indeed, it has been our spiritual conversations that have resourced me beyond measure. There are very few people in my world with whom I can have these conversations and her knowledge of universal principles has been incredibly valuable.

I am never made to feel crazy as she too enjoys a strong connection with Spirit. She intrinsically recognises there is a divine plan at work, with our role being to sit in trust and be guided for our highest good. We can be our true selves—authentic, flawed, optimistic, pessimistic, full of despair and full of hope together. We can be real. That's an incredible foundation for friendship and one I love and cherish.

Alex and I began as flatmates in the early 2000s, sharing a fabulous penthouse overlooking the Sydney skyline. We thoroughly relished our single days dancing in the nightclubs; we even enjoyed a few double dates! She has faced considerable health challenges in the last few years and has done so with incredible bravery, resilience and determination. Despite her considerable challenges she'd always find the strength to call and check in on me.

She was incredibly supportive of the decisions I was making as she recognised the changes—although devastating—were necessary for me to move forward in my truth. I have loved having Alex in my life, and although due to distance we don't catch up as often as we'd like, when we do it's as if no time has passed. That's true friendship. I just love her to bits.

My parents, Tom and Robyn, have been incredible in their care, love, devotion and constant support of me. Sure, we've faced challenges in our relationship at different times, but I have been so incredibly blessed. I really did win the parental lottery at birth.

I remember so clearly the day I relayed the story of meeting Jason to Mum. I was beyond excited to share my experience. We were standing on the deck by the pool with a glass of wine in hand. She listened with keen interest, even wonder (and probably a healthy dose of incredulity), as I explained how in a matter of hours my life changed forever.

Before I left for Margaret River my life was firmly and determinedly heading west. When I returned, a mere few days later, my life was heading east. I remember the very first words Mum uttered in response to hearing my story: "Right, what do we do now?" Without hesitation or judgement, she, in that one question, affirmed her commitment to me and my future.

I didn't realise it then, but she had known for some time that my marriage—although comfortable, safe and secure to a dependable, caring man—was not meant to be sustained into the future. She knew it before I did. She had been patiently waiting for me to have the courage to face the reality too. She didn't know the decision would be revealed by an encounter with a tall, dark and handsome man, but knew I would get there, somehow, in the end.

It took a little longer for Dad to accept my decision and I completely understand and appreciate his perspective. He is a dedicated and deeply devoted Roman Catholic who holds the institution of marriage in the highest regard. He was raised in an era where separation and divorce were not in God's plan, an era where you saw relationships and commitments through to the very end. He could also see the impact my decision would have on his grandchildren and this broke his heart.

He eventually understood why I made the decision. I remember the conversation clearly. We were sitting together in my apartment, sharing a bottle of shiraz, when I asked if he was ready to hear my story. He said yes. So, I read him the first draft of the first chapter of this book—basically the notes I had written on the back of my itinerary in the hotel room in Margaret River after my morning walk with Jason.

I stole a few glances at his face while he took in my story, hoping to find understanding in his warm, caring blue eyes. I finished reading and waited patiently for his response.

On some level I was looking for acknowledgement, on some level I was seeking affirmation, but most importantly I was craving acceptance. Recognition and acceptance that he finally understood I didn't have a choice if I were to be true to myself, true to my future.

The mere seconds he spent choosing his words felt like a lifetime. Gently placing his hand on mine, he finally spoke: "I can only imagine how hard that must have been." Receiving his understanding that evening meant the world to me.

The most important person to acknowledge, be thankful for and grateful to is my ex-husband. (On consultation, he decided he'd like to be known as Brad!) A man who thought everything was fine and was travelling quite effortlessly through life with his wife and children. A man who had thrust on him such a dramatic decision it changed his world overnight. He didn't see it coming. Nor could he have prevented it.

I didn't give him a choice of whether or not to end our relationship. I made the choice for us both. I made the choice to separate myself from him and in doing so prevented our daughters from receiving full-time care from both their parents.

Yet even under these most challenging of circumstances Brad managed the transition with resigned acceptance. He created no unnecessary drama. He put our children first and has, to this day, taken such incredible care of them. They are blessed to have him as their father.

I am incredibly lucky to have him in my life, fulfilling such an important role. We are friends and we are a team for our gorgeous girls.

Releasing

My sadness has stemmed from the fact that some very old friends, along with some friends who had been in my social circle for a few years, have for all intents and purposes left my life. Friendships that survived my 20s and 30s, that I assumed would be with me forever, haven't survived. Friends made in the neighbourhood, for whom Brad and I hosted dozens of parties and celebrations over the years, just disappeared.

I have spent a lot of time wallowing in the emotions of resentment, incredulity and sadness over my changing friendship landscape. The waters were choppy and sometimes even cyclonic. I had to swim from one end of the beach to the other by myself—one painful stroke at a time. But the insights into myself and all my relationships during this incredibly difficult time were almost revolutionary. Remember though, hindsight is wonderful.

I certainly didn't foresee that certain friends wouldn't be there for me when I needed them the most. I maybe even took it for granted that they would be there, holding my hand. When they weren't, it felt like a cruel betrayal. It was heartbreaking. It took an enormous amount of effort to accept this new reality, especially in the midst of what was already a spiritual upheaval—the likes of which I'd never experienced.

After Brad and I separated, there was not one invitation for a drink or BBQ from some very old friends or our neighbourhood friends, even though our hospitality as a couple over many years had been generous. We had made it clear that we were very happy to continue to socialise together, but not one invitation was forthcoming. This brought sadness into both of our lives.

I workshopped this with a few single girlfriends and found they had experienced similar treatment. Suspicions ranged from "she's no longer part of a couple, and we only socialise with couples" to "I don't want to take sides" to "I don't want my other friends to be uncomfortable" to "she's single now and could steal my husband" to "I didn't really like them much anyway, just loved their parties". Of course, there are probably many other reasons, but a few of these resonated with my group of single friends.

I now acutely understand the pain this causes so I make this promise to my friends: if you ever go through a devastating change in life, whatever that may be, I will be there by your side for as long as you need me to be there for you.

The more pressing and heartbreaking work was how to comprehend, assimilate and then finally accept that certain long-term friends, who were very dear to me, were leaving my sphere. I never believed I would have to face this situation. In order to accept this new reality, I needed to recognise that quite simply and in the most complex of ways, the healing had to come from within. From my soul. I needed to be vulnerable and brutally honest.

At the same time I was grappling with this evolving friendship landscape, I was guided to find a podcast discussion on Molly McCord's YouTube channel between Molly and Erica Elmuts titled *Venus, Friendship and Divine Feminine Healing Themes*. Talk about timing—thank you, angelic team!

They discussed the changing relationship landscape from an energetic perspective. As we evolve—awaken—become more our true selves, we begin to vibrate at a different energetic frequency. An energetic disconnection with others happens and our mental selves can't figure it out. We begin to flounder and ask all the questions. What's wrong with me? Why don't they want to spend time with me anymore? Why do I feel heavy when I think about them? Why don't I want to reach out and plan that next coffee catch-up?

When I considered these questions—when my logical mind couldn't understand this vibrational disconnect—intense feelings of loneliness, exclusion and confusion emerged. Sadness, grief and even anger bubbled to the surface, demanding to be acknowledged and then mindfully released. There were many tears.

I also considered another perspective. Were these friends just further along on their own journey of awakening? Perhaps they had been kindly and patiently assisting my spiritual growth all along, understanding it was now time to step back and allow me to elevate on my own. This perspective demanded humility, compassion and gratitude for those who had been an integral part of my life, but have since left my friendship circle.

I decided to make peace with these transitions by taking responsibility for my behaviour. When it became clear it was time for some friends to move on, I consciously sent them on their way with my love and blessings for a wonderful future. Over time, I have come to a place not only of understanding but acceptance of the loss of some friendships. It is still sad, sure, but I move forward anyway.

One of the changes you may be feeling right now
is that you want to be with people who SEE you –
the real you, all of you, those who get your FULLNESS.

It's no longer about hangin' with peeps you know
just because you know them or have been in their lives for years;
it's being with those who understand
all of your layers and dimensions.

They SEE your journey with deeper eyes
Molly McCord

I believe people come into our lives for a reason, a season and occasionally a lifetime. Sometimes a season can be months, sometimes a season can last for decades. Just because a relationship isn't meant to last a lifetime, it's important to acknowledge, cherish and sit in gratitude for the fun times and the soul growth it delivers.

Happily, some souls who left my sphere early on have found their way back to me, but I no longer hold on to them as tightly. I think this is a great lesson too. It doesn't just apply to these souls, it applies to everyone who touches my life. I enjoy the time and energy I spend with people and have gratitude for the part they play in the tapestry of my life. I also look forward with joyous anticipation to the energetically aligned souls who will show up and not only accept me, but emphatically rejoice in my strength, courage, bravery— even audacity!

This awakening journey has increased my dependence and trust in myself. I have recognised I am, ultimately, all I need in this world. That doesn't mean for a minute I don't relish and treasure the company of others. Certainly not. I thrive on intimacy on all levels. But previously, I believed I needed people in my life to survive. I understand now that I don't.

I love the relationships I have but recognise the most critical and enduring relationship I have, and will ever have, is with myself. I am the one person I can unfailingly rely on. I am the one person who will always have my back. I am my own best friend. I am my own soulmate.

Attracting

It follows perfectly that when some people leave our lives we attract new ones for the next part of our journey. That is what has happened to me. Quite unconsciously, with no intent and zero effort. As the expression goes, "Nature abhors a vacuum."

My way of expressing this concept is "the universe abhors a vacuum". I believe it is precisely because we shared no history that it was easier to go deep—and go deep quickly—with these new souls. I am so grateful for these new friends in my life. I can be my authentic self, as I am now, without the baggage of the past.

My second Hunter Valley retreat experience and another reason it was so wonderful for me was meeting a new friend Jackie.

Jackie is a vivacious, charismatic, ambitious and extremely competent career woman with a real zest and energy for life. She's fit, attractive, has an easy smile and a laugh that's incredibly infectious. She has endured many relationship challenges and has moved through and healed these with grace and positivity. I delight in her company and look forward to every hike, brunch and crazy disco diva event I can drag her along to!

She said the sweetest thing to me over dinner one night. She said she loves who she is when she is with me. That I bring out her fun side, her inner child, and I make her fond of herself.

Wow, those words immediately gave me goosebumps. I feel the same way every time I see her!

We not only laugh till our bellies hurt, we speak honestly when there is a truth required to be communicated (and it may not always be easy to hear), yet always speak from our heart in our cocoon of love and authentic friendship. We consciously and determinedly support each other's growth and evolution every step of the way. She has been a role model for me, and I am incredibly appreciative for her continued guidance and support. I am so lucky to call her my dear friend.

I have also learnt that not all people who cross my path will become friends, and that's completely okay. I try them on and have the confidence to let them go if we are not communicating on the same level. There is opportunity for personal growth from every interaction if I'm open to it. I've also recognised it's not necessarily for my growth either—it can sometimes be for them, and just for them.

A small interaction—whether it's saying "good morning" on

public transport or holding a door open—has the potential to help someone move through something heavy or light, or it may just add to the colour of their day.

I've even had a few experiences with people that left me feeling disappointed and sad for the relationship it could have been. Again— and hindsight and perspective are wonderful—it's been a learning adventure. I do my best not to dwell on these people. Instead I release them, let them go. There are truer and more authentic connections to be made and enjoyed in the world.

I had one such learning adventure with a man I met on the Argentina trip.

Paul and I were not immediately drawn to each other but that changed. It's a case of an intense encounter where it took time and energy for me to process the connection I felt with him, and ultimately find peace and acceptance of the outcome.

I never felt any real sexual attraction to him, as cute and fit as he was. He certainly didn't look twice at me in that way either. Nonetheless, I gravitated to him and found myself lost in his presence. I was drawn to him, and I believe he was drawn to me too. We would find ourselves sitting together, so engrossed in conversation it felt like there was no one else in the room. But there were 12 others sitting in the hotel lounges in El Calafate and El Chalten in the heart of Patagonia enjoying boisterous conversation and bottles of malbec also.

But I didn't see or hear anyone else. I was completely focused on Paul and he was completely focused on me. We were in our own intense bubble and it was delicious. I felt genuinely at ease, completely safe and totally able to be myself. We would find ourselves engaging in deep and meaningful conversations usually reserved for close friends with years of shared history. It was wonderful—yet it was challenged.

I wasn't his romantic choice, yet for me it didn't matter. I confess though, I found myself constantly fighting the desire to be close to him, to spend time with him and build a connection. And the universe had ways of bringing us together, just as I desired, despite my (half-hearted) attempts to stay away. We would find ourselves sitting next to each other at dinner, in the back of the mini-bus sharing headphones and favourite tunes, and working out the next day's travel arrangements together.

I had to contemplate though, was this connection just in my head? I consulted a few of the women in our group. They were unanimous—it was obvious to them we shared a unique rapport.

The trip ended in the early hours of the morning in the Buenos Aires airport. All of us were physically exhausted and emotional. The end of the holiday was fraught with difficulties (airline related, not Flash Pack related). I even resorted to sleeping on the floor of a regional airport in the middle of Patagonia—behaviour I had managed to avoid my whole life up until that point!

Paul and I embraced, sharing a heartfelt goodbye. I was sad to leave him. We promised to see each other in Melbourne the following month. I left Argentina believing our connection showed promise for a solid friendship built on genuine compatibility and enjoyment of each other's company.

So what happened? Why is he no longer in my life? It's a question I spent some time considering.

It wasn't that our Melbourne rendezvous wasn't good—on the contrary, it was delightful. We sat for hours drinking malbec in a crowded bar with fun and frivolity surrounding us, talking—again—as though no one else were present. He walked me back to my hotel, sent me to my room with a kiss on the cheek and a promise to reconnect in Sydney the following month.

But we didn't. He didn't make time for me that trip, or the following trip I made to Melbourne.

I had to let him go. I had evolved to the point where I just wouldn't chase. I won't chase a connection—friendship or potentially romantic —that is not reciprocated. By this time, I had realised that people don't always stay in your life.

It does make me a little melancholy, as I believe our connection was worth investing in. But he didn't, and that is okay. People come into your life for a reason, a season, occasionally a lifetime.

What has delighted me is another Aussie from the trip has become a good friend. We don't see each other often, but I look forward to and thoroughly enjoy our catch-ups reminiscing on our amazing adventure. I didn't appreciate him like I should have on the trip. On reflection, I recognise how kind and thoughtful he was towards me. He really thought about me. When he could see I was struggling, he was the first to offer his arms for a cuddle. He remembered I loved a particular malbec we enjoyed with dinner one evening, so when I was sick he went into town and bought a bottle for me.

When we arrived home, he called with an invitation to an evening of Argentinian wine tasting. It brings a smile to my face when I think of him. Plus, let's be honest, it certainly doesn't hurt that he is also tall, dark and handsome! Oh, and his name is Ash—he wanted you to know!

Reason Season Lifetime

People come into your life for a reason,
a season or a lifetime.
When you figure out which it is,
you know exactly what to do.

*When someone is in your life for a **REASON**, it is usually*
to meet a need you have expressed outwardly or inwardly.
They have come to assist you through a difficulty,
to provide you with guidance and support,
to aid you physically, emotionally or spiritually.
They may seem like a godsend, and they are.
They are there for the reason you need them to be.

Then, without any wrongdoing on your part
or at an inconvenient time, this person will say or do something
to bring the relationship to an end. Sometimes they die.
Sometimes they walk away.

Sometimes they act up or out and force you to take a stand.
What we must realise is that our need has been met,
our desire fulfilled; their work is done.
The prayer you sent up has been answered
and it is now time to move on.

When people come into your life for a **SEASON,**
it is because your turn has come to share, grow or learn.
They may bring you an experience of peace or make you laugh.
They may teach you something you have never done.
They usually give you an unbelievable amount of joy.

Believe it! It is real! But only for a season.

LIFETIME *relationships teach you lifetime lessons;*
those things you must build upon in order to have a solid emotional
foundation. Your job is to accept the lesson,
love the person/people (anyway), and put what you have learned to
use in all other relationships and areas of your life.
It is said that love is blind but friendship is clairvoyant.
Brian A. (Drew) Chalker

5.
Looking for Love
in All the Wrong Places

Like many, I have been conditioned that to be whole, it is necessary to be in a relationship. For better or for worse, the culture of 'grow up, get married and have children' is deeply embedded in my psyche. Indeed, I wasn't *complete* without a partner.

Although I have enjoyed periods of singledom, I've always been more comfortable with someone in my life. I love nothing more than sharing stories of our day whilst cooking dinner together, enjoying some red wine and cheese, and snuggling up on the couch.

As a woman with a healthy interest in emotional intimacy, I recognised an important part of my future would include building relationships with others. My experiences with a few men over the last few years have highlighted the qualities most important to me and clarified who I want to be in a relationship. These men have been an incredibly important part of my journey, providing ample opportunity for self-awareness, personal-growth and ultimately, self-acceptance.

First, There Was Aiden

Aiden is a tall, fit and charming man with an incredibly seductive voice, perfect white teeth and the bluest of eyes. We met quite by accident (divine intervention?) whilst I was eating dinner alone at a fabulous Asian restaurant. We engaged in stimulating conversation and enjoyed many laughs over some (bottles of) riesling. As we left the restaurant late in the evening, he whispered into my ear, "I'd like to see you again." I was thrilled as I usually travelled solo on business trips and engaging company over dinner sounded delightful.

A few months later we met for an after-work drink. Our rendezvous took place at a cosy, dimly lit, impossibly cool small bar where we shared a bottle of pinot noir and a cheese plate. I dispensed quickly with the surface level chit-chat.

I had just met Jason and was beyond eager for a male's perspective of my experience. I could be completely open and truthful with him as he knew no one I was speaking about.

It was such a relief to have this delicate conversation with someone who could sympathise, and it certainly didn't hurt that I was attracted to him. I briefly considered he might have been looking at me in that way too, but I quickly dismissed it. Jason was the only man I could possibly consider in my future, of that I was certain.

The night was fabulous. We enjoyed lots of wine and energising conversation. His initial reaction to my story was one of incredulity, but over the course of the evening he became as convinced as I was that I should pursue this connection with determination. He too believed I had met 'the one'. The evening ended after midnight with him walking me back to my hotel lobby, sending me to my room with a kiss on the cheek and body-embracing hug. It was perfect.

Aiden introduced me to WhatsApp, and we enjoyed continuous, private communication over the next few months. Our banter was a constant source of entertainment and a welcome distraction from what was going on in my life.

On my next business trip we met at the same bar. It had been months since our last get-together and by this time, everything in my world had changed. I had left my husband, the family home was sold, I had moved to a fabulous apartment, and the girls and I were adjusting to our new reality. I had exchanged those first few emails with Jason, and I was trying to move forward with my life. I was doing my best to open myself up to new opportunities.

I had also begun to wonder if there was genuine chemistry developing between Aiden and me, or if he was merely a gorgeous distraction from my thoughts of Jason which were, at the time, still all-consuming. It was time to find out.

I sat down and wrote a brief note in my diary just before our catch-up:

There is nothing to lose with broaching the idea of taking things further and only ego at stake. I can handle that. My true desire is to be open and honest with myself and my feelings. I move forward with inner strength and confidence in my new life and completely trust the universe to deliver what I require at the right time.

We sat at the bar, facing each other. Our legs were intertwined, which ensured more than a little physical contact. We were very close. There was nowhere to look except into his delicious, piercing blue eyes. The only break, when our connection became too intense, was the glass of pinot noir. Having spent more than a little time dreaming of this evening, I had decided that if it felt right on the night, I would be brave and turn the heat up a notch.

I felt it. The electricity and desire on both sides was obvious. I looked directly into his eyes and confessed my attraction. I stood embraced him, and kissed his cheek. Then, with his arms tightly wrapped around my waist that I took as a sign of his reciprocal interest, I made my way around his cheek to his lips.

Boom! We didn't separate for the next three hours. We held hands, kissed, laughed, kissed, embraced, kissed some more and drank lots of wine. The night ended when we were asked to leave the bar at closing time. I felt like I was in my early twenties again. He walked me back to my hotel and went home.

A social event was our next engagement and, after yet more months of texts and innuendo, my sense of anticipation was high.

I had been upgraded to a magnificent suite in my five-star hotel—

clearly a sign the room would be shared with another. I was ready. It was the holiday season, I was wearing a gorgeous dress, my hair was out, my makeup bright and I had a glass of champagne in hand.

The evening showed real promise. We would gravitate to each other often and enjoy fun, flirtatious and physically close conversation. Then he grabbed and held my hand whilst speaking with another couple. My heart skipped more than one beat. The end of the night drew near. At the eleventh hour though, after an evening of flirtation, he left the bar with an apologetic look and a short goodbye. I was deeply hurt.

When I returned to my hotel suite that evening, I was distraught. How did I misread the signs? How did I misread his intentions? How did I get it wrong for so many months? I asked my Wisdom of the Oracle cards *"In my highest good, and the highest good of all, what is the single message I need to receive at this time in relation to Aiden?"*

OBSERVER

Essential Meanings: *Perspective; objectivity; neutral observation from a distance.*

Hmm, perhaps it was time to take a step back and breathe. *"Most people see the world through a personal lens. They closely identify with their feelings and experiences—so much so that they come to believe these are the only reality."*

The message rang true, clear as a bell. It was time to observe and consider not only my behaviour, but critically evaluate Aiden's behaviour from a more neutral vantage point.

It was time to step back and really acknowledge the truth of my 'relationship' with Aiden. He never asked for me to be in his life in any other capacity than as friends. He didn't pursue me. I pursued him, and I was determined. Yes, there was flirtation. Yes, we shared a few kisses. But he never initiated, only I did. I put so much pressure on Aiden and me working in the way I wanted it to work, which was of course the only way our temporary relationship should unfold, that he began to pull away.

This was certainly an emotionally dangerous time for me, or more accurately, for my fragile ego and sense of self-worth. I just didn't know if I was capable of handling (another) rejection. Then it finally dawned on me as I lay in my luxurious (and empty) king bed with the sounds of the city humming below: I was transferring my desire for Jason on to Aiden. I was looking to Aiden to save me.

On returning home from the trip, I was aching and miserable.

I consulted my Archangel Oracle cards, and before I could even begin to shuffle, one card flew right out of the deck. It was Angel Therapy. I didn't need to read the card's message in the booklet; my inner voice firmly delivered the message. "Let him go." Being slow on the uptake, my inner voice repeated the phrase to ensure the message penetrated my soul: "Let. Him. Go." But I couldn't do it. I just couldn't do it.

During that time my ability to see, think or make clear decisions was absent. I played it cool at times and desperate at others. I felt a sense of entitlement to his company that was completely unfair to him and he quite rightly stepped back.

Why was I struggling to trust my intuition? The direct messages from both Aiden and my oracle cards had been so clear! Let. Him. Go. So why was it proving so difficult?

My diary notes about the relationship with Aiden are confronting to read. There is so much emotion in my language. I feel very protective of Amanda then. The Amanda in my diary showed courage and audacity—but also held within her fear, sadness and loss.

About 12 months after meeting Aiden, I wrote about the lessons I had learned from our experience:

I have begun to understand what is truly important to me in any relationship:
- *Communication is key for me*
- *Both parties need to feel appreciated, valued and respected*

- *There needs to be equal give and take*
- *Spending time together is most important to me*
  —to feed and grow a connection
- *I want so much to talk to someone on a deep level*
  —I want to spend hours and hours talking together
- *I am intense and I need to go deep and that's okay*
  —the right person will love that quality of mine.

Aiden and I have graciously left each other's orbit. The break-up (using the term super loosely) wasn't easy—it took me three times to see it through, to not go back for more pain. Sounds quite sadistic, doesn't it? I have spent much time reflecting on my experience and now look back with gratitude for his immense contribution to my recovery.

It was confronting. It was exciting, excruciating and embarrassing. It was delightful. And it was aligned.

People come into your life for a reason, a season, sometimes a lifetime. Aiden was a reason and a season. Aiden supported (and tolerated) me through the most unstable, challenging and emotional time of my life. Though we are no longer connected, I wish him everything he dreams of, everything he desires, everything he deserves.

Then Along Came Luke, Again

First, we have to go back to the early 2000s. I was a young and single professional enjoying the financial services industry in Sydney. Companies had plenty of money to spend, and I was happy to spend it for them. I was smart, ambitious and loved to socialise. I was in the right place at the right time. There were many multi-day conferences to attend with perks of beautiful hotels, sublime dinners and incredible bespoke experiences.

I have a particularly fond memory of a conference in Melbourne where, once the work was complete, we were hosted at the Spring Racing Carnival. The Derby Day Event is a highlight of the racing year. Tickets are highly sought after and you need connections (and money) to experience the lavishness of the day.

At this event, I encountered a tall, dark and handsome man who immediately turned my head. Fun and flirtation ensued. The connection was intense, the attraction was red hot. I have a saucy memory of us sitting together at the back of the bus as we headed to our five-star hotel at the end of the race day. He was graciously tying up the spaghetti straps on my summer dress, enticingly close to my strapless bra, as we swapped numbers to meet up later.

We didn't meet up that evening but made the most of every opportunity over the next few months to spend time together. Financial services at the start of the new century provided a constant stream of extravagant events that delivered cocktails, dance floors and plenty of opportunity for flirtation.

One night we found ourselves facing the chemistry that had been building between us head-on. I was on the dance floor with a man more senior than me, whose behaviour had become inappropriate, when I realised I was feeling decidedly uneasy. It took only a glance over to Mr Tall, Dark and Handsome (who happened to be watching from the sideline) for him to take control. He immediately swept in and offered a few choice words to my dancing companion before escorting me away from my uncomfortable situation.

As we walked out of the club together, we were finally offered the perfect opportunity to explore a real beginning. I was nervous but excited. I loved being in his company. He drew me in, and I was ready to jump—two feet first. But instead of asking me for dinner, or drinks, or a walk in the park, he decided to proposition me with a hotel room and fireworks. I remember the line well: "Let me take you to a hotel and give you the best sex of your life!" I was shocked, I was upset and I went home immediately.

A good friend of mine suggested I should have countered with

"Let's see, I'll let you know how you rated in the morning." I would never have been that quick-witted, but in any case, it is not how I would have replied, even if I was that clever!

For me, emotional connection and sexual intimacy have always gone hand in hand. When it comes to a man I see potential with, I take it slowly.

That was the case with Luke. I saw real potential in us, and I wasn't going to throw the opportunity of a potential future away on one night of passion. I wanted more.

It is why I was so incredibly upset with how the evening ended. I was as upset with myself as I was with him, perhaps more. I had clearly misread all the signals over many months. I had completely misread his intention. I had, in my naivety, assumed the chemistry we shared had real promise, that it had the potential for a relationship, the potential for a future together.

Until that experience, I had always trusted my judgement, my gut, my intuition—my internal guidance and navigation system.

This time was different. This time my intuition failed me, and it hurt. It struck me in my core. My intuition—that Luke liked me and wanted to move forward in a relationship with me—was spectacularly wrong. This was a real turning point, a tower moment in my relationship with myself. The faith, trust and understanding I had always enjoyed with myself had been broken. I went on to carry this sense of not really trusting myself or trusting my internal judgment, guidance or intuition for the next 15 years.

I was at a party one night, about 12 months after meeting Jason, and there was Luke again.

He and I had chatted awkwardly over the years, him calling me "mate" and usually taking the first opportunity presented during any social situation to leave my company. I had become accustomed to this behaviour, no longer taking it to heart. Our relationship was strained and I had accepted this as fact a long time ago. I found myself chatting (again awkwardly) with him and a mutual friend, when our friend confessed I had come up in conversation over the years as a woman who had turned a few heads in their circle.

It was genuinely fascinating and somewhat embarrassing to me as I never thought I would be someone of interest. I was never in the cool group, never in the social cliques that developed and never the all-night party girl. And then something even more incredulous happened.

Luke confessed he had hit on me once and got "shot down in flames". What?! Clearly our recollection of events was distinctly different! Although I had declined his hotel room and fireworks proposal, so perhaps it's true for him? I was completely thrown by this proclamation, so a few minutes later when he abruptly left (in his usual manner), it was a relief. About ten minutes later he came back to the bar and walked straight up to me. He apologised for leaving without a proper goodbye and suggested we have lunch. I nodded in stunned agreement.

Fast forward a month or so, with no communication from him, let alone an invitation to lunch, I ran into him in a coffee shop. Pleasantries ensued over the next few minutes (his use of the term "mate" was back), but I was feeling bold and reminded him of our last conversation.

"It's fine if you don't want to see me for lunch as you suggested, but I'm not one for an elephant in the room—I'm too old for that. So if you have something to say, just say it." An invitation for drinks after work was immediate and we were in play for that evening.

We met in a dark speakeasy and a bottle of pinot noir was ordered. It was mere minutes before the conversation took a dramatic turn. He confessed he had thought about me over the years and was wholly apologetic about the immaturity of his response after I declined his hotel room invitation. He said he was angry and hurt, interpreting my response as a total refusal of him. It was the most unanticipated revelation.

Upon regaining my composure, I explained his offer was not communicated as an opening to a relationship—far from it! He had hurt me greatly that night and in the few attempts I made to get us back on track the following month or so. I confided I had felt a genuine connection with him and thought there was real promise in us. To give myself a much-needed reprieve, I hailed our waiter. It was time for another bottle of wine.

The admissions continued for the next hour. He was emphatic that I was his lost opportunity and he took full responsibility for us not ending up together. He confided that he called me mate to keep me at a distance—his protection mechanism. Further, he had deliberately avoided me when he could. I was shocked, I was speechless, but most of all I was saddened. Saddened for what might have been.

The evening ended with him revealing he would be jealous of the man I end up with. He understood I was in a great place in my life. I had a future where I could get everything I wanted, needed and deserved in a partner. But it wasn't going to be possible with him. He admitted he was in a relationship and had been for many years.

It was time for the evening to end. Time for me to go home and process this completely unexpected revelation on my own, in the sanctity of my private, calm space. My evening diary note is alarming in its accuracy:

Amanda, this is the most perfect outcome. It is your closure. You have been seeking this for many years and you have it. It is perfect and it is complete. Don't think about a future together. There isn't one. Be happy and content with this outcome.

We caught up one last time at yet another cool, dimly lit bar to have a final conversation. I wasn't expecting a different outcome, but nonetheless, I was nervous.

However, I was becoming more comfortable with my connection to Spirit, so I chose one card from my Wisdom of the Oracle deck the morning of our last meeting. I received:

TIME TO GO

Essential meanings: *Endings; completion; walking away from something because there is nothing else to learn or experience.*

That message was not at all ambiguous! We enjoyed a few drinks and some lighter banter our last evening together, but the conversation revealed nothing new. I reflected on the message: *"There is nothing left for you to do, be or experience in your present circumstances. Take the risk and move on even if you need to be in transition for a time. Your destiny is calling you."*

The message was crystal clear. There was nothing new to experience with Luke. In reality, the evening only served to prolong the inevitable goodbye.

As I made my way home on the ferry, I felt the sadness and grief of what might have been but reread the relationship message from TIME TO GO:

'Although this card could speak to a break-up, drifting apart or the end of a soul contract, it is more about release than destruction. Remember the saying "If you love something, let it go. If it comes back, it's yours. If not, it never was." Endings are always a sign of new beginnings. If you want something deeper, walk away.'

I craved something deeper in my heart and in my soul. I had found the courage to acknowledge what I truly wanted, and I was now strong enough to walk away on my own terms.

I did some research into karmic relationships and on many levels the information seemed to fit. In a karmic relationship there is often an instant connection but they frustrate you from the beginning—there are often a lot of misunderstandings early on. That was certainly true for Luke, but nonetheless I sought greater understanding, pondering additional questions: Why, after all these years, did he throw an emotional grenade into my lap that took me time to defuse and left abrasions all over me? What was the higher purpose of our re-engagement? There had to be one, surely.

The 'ah-ha' hit like a lightning bolt. I laughed and I cried. I recognised his final gift. It was incredible. It was profound. Life changing and life fulfilling. His gift to me was this: The answers I seek reside inside me. It is about my intuition. It is about trusting in myself. I finally recognised what he took from me—or I let him take from me—was trust and faith in my internal guidance system, my intuition, my connection with my soul.

I hadn't been wrong all those years ago. He did have strong feelings for me and wanted us to be together. He had wanted to move forward with our connection. He wanted to explore a future with me as much as I did with him. I hadn't misread the signals after all. I had read them correctly. I exhaled.

I am grateful for Luke's re-entry into my life at a time when I could recognise, comprehend and integrate the lessons. He gifted me the ability to reconnect with my trust in my intuition. My very soul.

By coming back into my life, he opened the door for me to confidently trust me for the first time in many years.

My Online Dating Experiment

Whilst navigating the treacherous waters of Aiden and Luke and a few other men who presented themselves unexpectedly for a dinner or two, I also experimented with online dating.

It wasn't an option before I married so I had no experience meeting potential partners in this way. Dating in the 1990s and early 2000s seemed much easier. You would meet potential suitors the old-fashioned way: in a bar, at house parties, through friends of friends or at work. For me, it was mostly through work as that's where I spent most of my time.

In my industry and the roles I gravitated towards, there were always plenty of social functions and opportunities for after-work drinks. I didn't find it overly challenging to secure an invitation for a date which meant I usually had a story or two to share with girlfriends over Sunday brunch which kept them thoroughly entertained—usually at my expense! I enjoyed my younger dating days and look back fondly at how willing people were to start an in-person conversation with a smile, wink or offer of a drink. Fast forward 15 years or so and boy oh boy, had the world changed!

I went into my experiment, I thought, quite mature and level-headed. You are never attracted to every person in a bar, so why should you be attracted to everyone on an app?

After some research into the dozens of dating apps, I decided to try Bumble first as I valued being able to make the first move. It put me in control of the conversation and ensured I did not receive undesirable advances. But it didn't work out so well for me. A few short texts, many ghosting experiences, and that was it. My first failed attempt.

I then dabbled on the RSVP site, rationalising (read: grasping) that anyone who is going to make a little effort to answer a few questions and articulate why they are looking for love online might be more my scene. But that didn't work out so well for me either. My profile was clearly not attractive or enticing as most of those I did approach with a wink or a smile clearly didn't consider me worthy of much banter or an actual meet. I considered this my second fail, or perhaps a repeat of the first one?

My girlfriends, however, enjoyed my foray into the world of online dating immensely. At every social engagement, I'd be coerced into handing over my phone for friends to swipe through profiles. They thoroughly relished living vicariously through their now single friend!

One glorious Sydney Sunday I was having lunch with a few girlfriends at a fabulous restaurant on the water. They were beyond excited to view the few potential suitors I had matched with and eagerly commandeered my phone. Whilst intently scrolling, judiciously evaluating the selected few, one profile stopped a girlfriend in her tracks. She looked at me with a mix of incredulity and alarm. Everyone went silent as we immediately knew something was up.

"Time to spill!" I screamed.

It turned out the one man I found quite engaging was an ex-husband of a friend of hers. Well, an ex-husband didn't sound too bad to me. I was, after all, an ex-wife! The story didn't end there, however. She went on to disclose that he was in a serious relationship with another woman and was even living with her! Let's just say that when I confronted him with this information, he quickly removed himself from the app and we never exchanged contact again. At that point I decided I had endured enough of the online dating scene and promptly removed myself from any further excruciating experiences and rejections.

I had heard the horror stories. Cringed at the things I had been told about how wretched online dating could be. So why did I pursue it? Well, there were a few reasons. I had assimilated (the untrue belief) early in life that a relationship would complete me, would make me whole; that, in order to be successful in my life, I had to have someone by my side. I had to tick all the boxes. As strong, fierce and capable as I was in so many other areas of my life, I still felt the pressure of having to prove I was worthy, and at the time, that translated to being wanted by a man.

I also felt the pressure to validate my decision to leave my husband, to somehow justify my decision by finding love with another soul. Finally, I felt compelled to respond in a tangible way to the inevitable questions of "Have you met anyone new?", "Are you dating?" or "Have you met the man of your dreams yet?" These questions came from well-meaning friends, colleagues, family and even clients. So sharing a few disastrous online dating stories adequately deflected attention away from my state of singledom.

Initially I didn't think this foray into online dating provided any deep and meaningful insights other than it probably wasn't the way

I was going to meet my future partner (at this time, at least, I've learnt to never say never). But on further reflection, I recognise there was knowledge and growth from this experience to be appreciated.

The universe was saying quite firmly no, or at least not right now. It was protecting me. If I hadn't listened to my intuition and had the courage to close down the apps, I am confident I would have found myself in a half dozen toxic relationships that would have depleted my energy and eroded my already fragile sense of worth. What became crystal clear during this time was that I still had much healing to do, and this was merely a tactic I was employing to delay the work I needed to do on myself.

I was extremely grateful for the insight, and proud that I had, after many years, begun to listen to my intuition.

Tim ... Really?

After 18 months of limited success engaging with the opposite sex, along came Tim.

Tim and I became friends when I first moved to Sydney, and although we were not close, we would catch up occasionally to chat about our professional lives. He worked in the city but lived quite a distance from where I had built my life. We shared a similar history of relationships and found ourselves separating from our spouses under eerily similar circumstances. The parallels in our lives were quite remarkable.

Our changed home situations meant we were able to catch up more frequently. We both benefited from being able to share segments of our story we just couldn't reveal to our separate social circles. It was certainly helpful for me to have a male friend I could talk to about the men who had come and gone from my life over the recent past as well.

We enjoyed each other's company and looked forward to our time together. Our connection strengthened. Whilst out together one night, a few months into our renewed friendship, he propositioned me. It wasn't for a relationship in the traditional sense. He was offering a way for both of us to re-engage with intimacy. A 'friends-with-benefits' arrangement.

As I was considering his proposal, which took me a few months, I asked the question: *In my highest good and the highest good for us both, what do I do about moving forward with this particular offer from Tim?*

The three-card reading from my deck Wisdom of the Oracle by Colette Baron-Reid guided my decision.

TRUTH BE TOLD

Essential meanings: *Honesty; accepting things at face value; coming out of denial; the willingness to be transparent; clarity of communication.*

NO PLACE LIKE HOME

Essential meanings: *Authenticity; coming home to yourself; feeling at home; arriving at a place where you just 'fit'; being comfortable in your own skin.*

HERE AND NOW

Essential meanings: *Being fully present in the moment; living one day at a time.*

Everyone will read the cards differently but for me, there was no confusion with Truth be Told. *"People tell you who they are very quickly if you're willing to listen."* Later that week we had a very open, heartfelt and transparent conversation about the nature of our pending relationship. We were both single and looking for intimate companionship. We communicated our truth and articulated what we needed at this time in our lives.

No Place like Home was clear for me too. *"Lovers, friends ... are at home in your life right now."* Tim's offer was authentic and based on the strong friendship we had established. Our fondness for each other was genuine and reciprocated. I was looking for a relationship that offered *"emotional safety, comfort and the best aspects of familiarity"* and he was offering what I desperately craved. For him, he would be receiving what he needed at that point in his life which was companionship, a relaxed arrangement and a trusted space for deeper conversations.

The final message of Here and Now concluded the reading and wow, was it spot on. Yes, I could *'yearn for a love affair (I) may not have right now'*, but I had to live in the present moment. I had to live one day at a time. *"Tomorrow is beyond your reach. Yesterday cannot return. The now is all that is available to you."* I had, after much heartache, adjusted to the reality that Jason was not returning to my life. I had to trust that I had everything I needed right now. And Tim was right there, in the now, clearly articulating his proposition.

I said yes.

Tim and I would spend hours talking on my couch, engaging in a level of emotional honesty I had not enjoyed for a long time. We had delicate, real and raw conversations that provided us both perspectives we hadn't been able to realise on our own.

We acknowledged the trauma we had caused our families but admired the fact we had found the courage to end marriages that were no longer in anyone's highest good. Our spouses were wonderful, but they were not the right people to be walking with into the future. The natural extension of this was that we were not the right people to be by their side for their future. They each deserved someone more aligned, as did we. It was the first time I consciously registered just how brave we both were. We recognised our internal strength of owning our truth, and this brought us closer together in admiration and trust.

He was also a great cuddler and I felt safe and cared for, enveloped in his muscular arms. Physical touch is so incredibly resourcing and my time with him made it abundantly clear how important this is to me. I loved waking up to a warm body beside me and although we both knew we were not meant to be together in the long term, we relaxed into our experience and enjoyed each other. We both benefited from our emotional and physical connection and I was so thankful to have waited for him to have this experience.

There was another reason I knew saying yes to Tim was the correct decision for me. I had asked the universe a few months before we rekindled our friendship to send me a friend I could trust to reintroduce me to a level of intimacy that would enable me to begin the process of moving forward. I sent my wish into the universe and I surrendered to trust. To be honest, I didn't really have any expectation the universe would deliver on such a wish. Who would it possibly be? Clearly not Aiden or Luke! I certainly did not have Tim—or anyone else, for that matter—in mind.

If your wishes are in your highest good and in alignment with the universe, be prepared to be surprised and delighted. I certainly was.

But it did have to end. We were clear in our communication about the nature of our relationship from the beginning and the boundaries were set. Still, when it came time for us (him) to explore the world of dating it was hard for me to cut the ties. He had been such a comfort and a confidant; I was quite willing to let our arrangement continue. I enjoyed our companionship, the honesty and authenticity of our communication, the sense of emotional and physical safety I felt when we were together. And yes, the intimacy.

But after a few intense months this arrangement was no longer serving us, and he recognised it before I did.

I was guided to consult my Archangel Oracle Cards.

COMPASSION – ARCHANGEL ZADKIEL

"Soften your heart with respect to this situation, and all the people involved, including yourself."

TAKE BACK YOUR POWER – ARCHANGEL RAZIEL

*"Use your God-given power and intention to manifest
blessings in your life."*

I wrote about it in my journal:

*It's time to go. I am leaking emotional energy and the signs
are there. He is pulling away and I am not oblivious to the
message. I am becoming uneasy and not feeling in my power.
I am becoming too dependent on our time together to fill an
emotional void in my life I am not filling for myself. He was
never my guy (nor I his girl), but he was the right man for
the experience.*

*He has done what I needed him to do for me—he has
allowed me to open up to intimacy in a trusted and safe way
and I am comfortable again in my sexual skin. But I am hurting,
and it will take some time to work through this. And that's
okay. I will honour my feelings and honour our time together.*

*I need to work on fulfilling my emotional needs on my own,
and not look for it in someone else. I need to come back into
myself and find my contentment and happiness within. I am
stronger now, so much stronger.*

*It's time to refocus on becoming my best self and growing
and expanding to ensure that when it is the right time, I will
connect with the soul who is best for me, and I for them.
I am capable and confident—I am whole and complete as I am,
with myself for company.*

*When we stop looking for someone to complete us,
we find completion in ourselves.
The purpose of relationship is not to have another
who might complete you, but to have another
with whom you might share your completeness*
Neale Donald Walsch

Tim helped me believe in myself again—my desirability, and that I was enough.

I was enough, just turning up and being me. With my home clothes on and no makeup he accepted me, he enjoyed being with me. He had seen me in various dress sizes over the years, through the challenges of adjusting to single life, and in my most vulnerable state as I shared the soul connection experience of meeting Jason.

I thank him for giving me the confidence to brave the world of intimate relationships and my dear wish is that the closeness we shared forever binds us in friendship and mutual trust. I hope I have been a positive part of his life's journey as well.

When it's the right time for us both my future partner and I will meet in a most unexpected way.

We will lock eyes, our souls will connect and we will know we are home. I know what it feels like now. I have released the desire of him being a certain person, of being tall, dark and handsome, and crucially, I have surrendered to the universe's timeframe.

He (we) will be worth the wait. Of that I am completely certain.

6.
The World
of Energy Healing

I am meeting and I am merging with the ocean of oneness within ...

There are a multitude of mainstream 'alternative' therapies available in this world to experience and enjoy. These therapies are not overly confronting for my logical brain—the logical brain that had been running the show most of my life. The other key advantage is they are not reliant on manufactured drugs—prescription or otherwise—which is important to me.

I had tried many ways to 'cure' myself over the years and was generous with my financial resources. The nutritionist would work on understanding my vitamin and mineral deficiencies, sending me home with supplements and potions. The beauty therapist would experiment with diverse skin treatments to cure my dull-looking skin. The massage therapist would perform various types of massage—Thai, remedial, Swedish, pressure point, or lymphatic—to relieve the muscular stress I carried in my body. And chiropractic treatments would work on my physical structure so I could bear the weight of the world I insisted on carrying.

These therapies offer tremendous benefits for overall health and I am grateful for the many opportunities I've had to explore them.

But were they enough to restore the energetic, happy, aligned Amanda of years past, or would I need to be brave and go where I had never gone before? Was there a modality that would not only ask me to be physically present, but honestly, vulnerably, authentically present with my emotions as well? A therapy that would take me deep into my emotional world and begin the process of healing from within?

In my quest to find the answers to these questions, I discovered two energy modalities which complement the other healing tools that I have incorporated into my personal practice—journalling, yoga, music, oracle cards, travelling, a gratitude practice, connecting with angels and spending time in nature.

Kinesiology

A few years before meeting Jason, I was struggling with chronic exhaustion. I was feeling emotionally numb and physically depleted. I had the nagging sense that my life was off track, but had excused this away as simply the compromises required to live a 'successful' life.

During a meeting with my nutritionist, I expressed my bewilderment that, though I felt like we were making some progress, I was still feeling persistently lethargic. She recommended that I seek out a practitioner of kinesiology—a non-invasive energetic healing therapy which uses muscle testing to monitor information about a person's well-being.

Kinesiology is based on the principle of Traditional Chinese Medicine (TCM) where there is no separation between the health of the mind, body and spirit. It aims to identify the root or underlying cause of an imbalance in order to resolve it. The cause could be nutritional, emotional, structural, psychological, energetic, spiritual or sometimes a combination of these. This subtle subconscious healing modality is assimilated in the body, the mind and the spirit over many months, perhaps years.

The idea of just sitting with a stranger and really going deep into fears and anxieties, relationships, financial stress and family discord sounded incredibly daunting to me at the time. I had always been more of the strong but silent type. To the outside world I would project as a woman who was competent and capable, perhaps even intimidating (a reflection of the Scorpio intenseness I've come to accept, and now love about myself). The fact I even made the appointment and showed up is testament to how deeply I was in distress. Not on a conscious level, but my subconscious was screaming for help.

My recollections of the early sessions with my incredible therapist Ghislaine are vague. I was unable to process or identify my progress from session to session. My logical mind was still firmly in control. Contrast a broken arm set in a cast—an obvious sign of the injury, then evidence of the healing when the cast is removed. This form of internal healing, however, is much more subtle.

I first needed to identify the core wounds holding me back, then allow the stuck, toxic energy to release physically, emotionally, mentally and spiritually in a way that honoured my own healing process. It required me to communicate with my inner self and trust in my subconscious healing abilities.

The session began with what can best be described as traditional talk therapy—we would sit and discuss what was going on in my world. Then I would lie on a table under a warm blanket, and be muscle tested. Acupressure points would be held, and stress release techniques performed. Often, I would enjoy sound therapy and EFT (emotional freedom technique, or 'tapping').

There were sessions of conscious connected breathing where I (silently) questioned the benefits of just breathing and how this was possibly assisting my healing. Little did I know.

I would go home in a calmer state, with some homeopathic remedies and vitamins when the muscle testing identified a deficiency. I would sleep well that night and for a time, a quiet confidence in myself would return.

Although I began working with Ghislaine well before my Margaret River experience, we hadn't connected one on one in years. She had taken time off and moved her practice to the other side of Sydney. I had gone back to work full-time after my second child so was, again, living life at a frantic pace.

After meeting Jason I was in deep distress and intuitively knew I needed to reconnect with her and kinesiology. After a particularly gruelling day at work, I raced, in my usual manner, to make the appointment on time. I was tired and emotional, and it wasn't until seeing her again did I realise how much I had missed her.

In the first one-on-one session a few months after meeting Jason, well ... let's just say I took the time to relay the story of meeting him in excruciating detail. At the end of the recount—including the part where I initially reached out and he said no—I shared my belief that although our reconciliation was delayed, in my mind, it would still happen. How could life possibly unfold any other way? I had found him. He had found me. We had found each other.

Ghislaine held my heart, held sacred space for me, then tenderly but firmly redirected my focus. She gently moved me out of the fantasy (delusional?) world I had created.

I remember the moment so vividly. I was lying on the table, under the warm blanket with my eyes closed, when Ghislaine asked me to recite the following mantra out loud:

> *"Even though Jason has decided not to move forward with me, I love and accept myself.*
> *Even though Jason has decided not to move forward with me, I love and accept myself.*
> *Even though Jason has decided not to move forward with me, I love and accept myself."*

I didn't understand this mantra. Why should I even consider not moving forward with him? He was my soulmate, after all. We were destined to be together in this lifetime, surely. But being the compliant, box-ticking woman I was, I did what I was told.

As I lay on the table, a clear vision of a heart about four foot high appeared on a podium. The heart was strangled in a thick, grey, concrete case. The heart couldn't breathe. In that instant I experienced acute tightness in my chest.

And then, without any warning, very real tears began to stream down my cheeks. As I refocused on the vision of the heart encased in concrete, the concrete began to crack. The concrete pieces crumbled and crashed to the floor. I had to remind my body to breathe—to physically move air in and out of my lungs—something it's supposed to do automatically. It took a few minutes (I think, I don't know) for all the pieces of concrete to fall to the floor. What remained was an unobstructed view of this beautiful red pulsing organ, bathed in white light. It filled my entire vision.

I cried an ocean of tears that session. That was the night, that was the first time I acknowledged it wasn't Jason who had hurt me. I had hurt myself.

I recognised I had to take full responsibility. For myself. For my life. For my way forward. I couldn't rely on him to save me. I had to save myself. It was the night I truly began the journey back to me. Back to my heart, back to my soul. Back to me becoming—for the first time in a very, very long time—me.

While gathering material for this book, I became curious about what this experience was like for Ghislaine, so I asked if she would be open to contributing her clinical perspective for this chapter. She immediately and enthusiastically said yes! I was overcome with gratitude.

I provided no guidance for any specific topic to be addressed. I wanted her narrative to be purely hers. Upon receiving her contribution, and as I absorbed her interpretation of my life, I cried —a lot. There were also many, many ah-ha moments.

Amanda reaches out: Determined and enthusiastic, she immediately seeks an appointment. She doesn't ask information about what therapy I am doing, how I am doing it, or how much it costs. Is she referred by someone, I ask her, thinking someone has filled her in on the details most people need to know before committing to having their lives dissected? No, she says, I have found you on the internet and I would like to book a time with you.

This is Amanda.

Amanda's first appointment: Amanda is tired, her head feels heavy, her stress levels are too high, her vitality is compromised. She feels sick and sluggish and it's not from the food she eats. The walk from her house to mine has been performed at a pace more suited to a marathon walker. Back home is her husband and her two young daughters. She has been married for eight years.

She has no idea how the session will go. She is here waiting, wondering about how to feel relief from the countable and unaccountable weight that is increasingly burdening her. She has a few too many kilos for her liking and a few too many unenthusiastic thoughts. She is aware some things need to change, and she is sitting in this chair in my practice for that reason.

Yes, I think, beautiful! Well done, Amanda! I honour your courage and willingness to take responsibility for your life. I thank you for choosing me to be the way, the guardian and the witness of your healing. May I be by your side guiding you gently, lovingly and compassionately, and may I in turn be guided and inspired each step of the way.

Our beginning together: What struck me most about Amanda is her incredible amount of energy even though her energy system is so depleted. She is running, literally, on adrenaline and is facing adrenal exhaustion. What keeps her autonomic nervous system aroused and prevents her from relaxing is the thought that she is not living the life she thought she would.

The emotions I pick up through muscle monitoring that are preventing her feeling better balanced and more enthusiastic about life are affecting her liver and spleen, the two main organs that are the detoxification pathways of the body. We know now why she can't lose weight regardless of her nutrition and exercise regime.

Self-disapproval, feeling discontented, guilty and angry are affecting her self-worth. Amanda is not happy with herself. She should have done better; she should have done more! Her main source of underlying stress is financial insecurity, yet she is earning a desirable income.

Amanda's entire nervous system is being hijacked by a trauma she lived at around age 12 when a financial event that was sudden, unforeseen and devastating to their life struck her family. Her parents didn't recover financially, and Amanda took on the task of financing their lives as soon as she earned an income.

In the meantime, her health, happiness, and well-being are compromised. She is fighting with herself. She would like to change careers but at the same time has dreams for a beautiful home on the beach. The trauma of not having this is creating havoc in her equilibrium. The disparity between the need for safety and the need to relax and to let go and let be is inconceivable. As a result, Amanda cannot be who she is or who she needs to be at this stage of her life.

The skin on her face is thick and makes her look like she is wearing a mask. The mask of who she thinks she has to be in order to survive.

This is Amanda.

Amanda decides to let go of work and take some time off. What a brilliant, brave and enormous decision. This decision is a leap of faith. It goes against her needs for survival. Her nervous system has started to relax, as Amanda knows she cannot continue to sustain stress levels of that magnitude. She is happy to give herself a go. To live a life where work doesn't feel like work.

Amanda's creativity is very healthy. She has so many incredibly good ideas. I sense working with her, and with how she receives the session, that she is a healer herself.

The break from her career unfortunately doesn't last. She goes back in and begins the cycle again. The financial insecurity and need to do it all herself, to not trust it can be any other way, has resurfaced.

I do not see Amanda for three years. I take a year off and move my practice to the other side of Sydney. Our journey together continues three years later.

Amanda comes to a group conscious breathing workshop. She has just met Jason, and in her typical way she comes, decidedly, to sort this out. By the end of the breathwork session, her decision is made. She is leaving her marriage and has organised and planned how and when to do it. A few months later, we resume our work together.

A spiritual birth: It often takes a difficult experience, a shocking event, an inability to sleep, lose weight, or to feel good to realise that there could be more to life than the way we are living it. Grief, insomnia, digestive issues, mental health issues, an irresolvable dispute with family, friends or co-workers might lead one to consult a therapist. It is this disguised way the universe shows you the path—leading you back to your inner wisdom and back to your original nature which is love, light and peace.

Jason: Her encounter with Jason is beyond anything she has ever experienced. Being in his presence makes her fond of herself. She discovers intimacy at a soul level. And falls deeply in love. She didn't know about that kind of love before. The depth, the softness mixed with the excitement of love, of authentic connection.

The sense that you have always known that person and that you can not only be who you are, but you can be who you didn't even know you were! The expansivity and magnitude of that love, she had never felt before! But here it is.

Sadly, Jason says no. This hurts so much—she feels helpless, desperate, distressed. Amanda's heart has been broken open and it hurts. It hurts that he is not choosing her. It hurts that now she really knows love, she has to let it go.

In the big picture and on a spiritual level we know he doesn't need to choose her for her healing to begin. Through her suffering she recognises that.

The work has been done. Amanda's heart is open. She now knows what love is. She uses the pain to transform and heal her heart. The pain is great, the nervous system is shaken. Fear, anger, loneliness and doubt are coming up in our sessions to be cleared.

Amanda the 'doer' is lost, as there is nothing she can do but accept this situation. This will require a total rewiring of her nervous system—from fear to love, from fighting to relaxing.

The healing is profound. Amanda is changed. She has softened, and has, in a way, landed on earth.

This is Amanda.

Self-care: Amanda knows how to take care of her needs. She has moved to a nice apartment, enjoys an infrared sauna, and eats only nutritious, detoxifying food. She is a new person, and it shows. Her face looks different, her face's complexion is clear. What looked like a mask and made her skin look thick and opaque has thinned to show the real Amanda. And she is radiant!

Now that the walls of protection around Amanda's heart have been shaken to destruction, thanks to Jason, Amanda's healing has taken a new direction. Amanda knows she needs to find herself. The shock has allowed for her spiritual birth. Her life is now starting with a new consciousness and awareness.

Her nervous system has relaxed enough for her to trust life and to trust that there is a bigger plan, a universe, some intangible energy that plays a role in her life, guiding her and helping her to heal. Amanda is now receiving the answers she was looking for when we started working together all those years ago.

The relationships: Aiden is part of the journey. They have wonderful conversations, lots of wine and a keen friendship. They play see-saw. When one wants to go deeper in the relationship, the other one holds back and vice versa. This is tiring and confusing for Amanda.

It makes her feel more alone and in need of real affection, not just playfulness. Amanda's goal is to be in a relationship. She believes a relationship with the 'right' man will define her, complete her, make her a better person. She is chasing the wind of feel good and this makes her feel bad because it is not authentic.

She is learning boundaries.
She is learning to be firm.
She is learning to become authentic.
She is learning to release control.
She is learning no love or relationship can be forced or organised.
Love is messy.

She will learn the same lesson with Tim. A friend with whom she has decided to have a sexual relationship in order to reconnect with her own sexuality. It works wonderfully well. They are both separated from their partners and organise to see each other regularly.

Amanda rediscovers her body and gets in touch with her femininity. Everyone wins, up until Tim starts a serious relationship with another woman. Amanda feels abandoned and betrayed, even though this was the pact they had made. Amanda will have to learn how to be with herself, no crutches.

Meeting Jason was the catalyst for the healing of the belief she cannot trust men, that she can't sit safely in a relationship. Through each relationship Amanda is looking at healing trust with men. Amanda got it right when she said that each man was taking her closer to herself and that they each carried an important lesson for her. Each man is showing her another way of accepting uncertainty.

She is learning a valuable lesson—the energy of love. The more you give, the more you receive. Amanda has no problem with giving love, the doubt is in her ability to receive it. This is what is healing.

Life will facilitate this teaching through relationships we have with others up until we get that the person we are waiting for is us. I love noticing how each time we love ourselves more, the outcomes in our lives change.

As Amanda's nervous system is relaxing, she can contemplate the possibility of having no amorous relationship in her life for now. Not being in a relationship was uncomfortable for Amanda and often her intention for the session was about being in the ideal relationship and finding the right person. To protect her from the devastation of not being with Jason.

Now what do you do when you know your client is focusing on an illusory perception? Nothing. You just wait patiently and support the person to realise on her own that actually the only relationship she needs to have is with herself.

And she did it.

The idea of the book is born.

The book: Amanda is hoping her book will serve as guidance for anyone looking for inspiration on their healing journey. And it will, because we are all on a healing journey.

The creation of the book is Amanda's quest for healing and knowing Amanda, this is only the beginning of her new life.

I am so grateful to Ghislaine. Kinesiology has been enormously emotional and confronting, but ultimately, cathartic and healing. I am incredibly grateful for that precious moment in time when it finally dawned on me—the big, red, pulsating heart is mine.

It belongs to me. I belong to me. And I am enough.

Transference Healing

I have treated myself to the services of a spunky facialist named Kylie for a few years who has admirably toiled to preserve any semblance of youthful skin. This was no easy task given I grew up in Australia, which has the highest rate of skin cancer in the world. I grew up on the beach and although I was never one to sunbake for hours on end, I certainly enjoyed more than my fair share of surf, sand and sun.

There was also a level of vanity to my sun indulgence in my youth as a tan made me look healthier and certainly leaner. On reflection, this should not have been a concern in my late teens and early twenties.

Kylie and I have enjoyed many honest conversations about our lives and relationships, our work woes and the challenges of living in a city that, although beautiful, is also expensive and can be cold-hearted.

Although we did not socialise outside of our beauty sessions, our relationship engendered trust, invited honesty, and was pleasurable and uplifting for us both. Our time together allowed us to quite literally ditch the perception that beauty was only skin deep. Sometimes Kylie was the therapist and sometimes the roles were reversed.

One session we were talking about our quest for personal growth and the modalities we had engaged with to facilitate our healing. During this conversation she relayed her experience with Transference Healing, an energetic frequency healing modality. Kylie described her session as being revolutionary in the way it helped release toxic energy, leaving her feeling a lightness in both body and soul. I was intrigued to say the least and had a sense in that very moment it would form part of my healing protocol in the future.

It was a good 12 months before I picked up the phone to explore Transference Healing. The embracing of kinesiology had been my first foray into a deeper healing modality and it required an openness to energy work, spirituality and the subconscious body. The practical elements of traditional talk therapy and supplements to heal the physical body, however, kept the logical part of my brain content to experiment. I was now hungry for maximum and accelerated soul growth and intuitively knew it was the right time to welcome an alternate approach.

Transference Healing attracts people who are ready to create transformational change in a new way. It is spiritual, but also practical. I just needed to be open and receptive. If my journey thus far had taught me anything, it was certainly that!

I had to acknowledge and accept the possibilities of past lives and karma, of energetic cords of attachment created in other lifetimes that were still connected in this lifetime, and the concept that we are multidimensional beings living just one of our experiences in human form on this planet at this time. The term 'suspension of disbelief' comes to mind, but at this point I was already open to the idea that there must be more. I felt confident and comfortable enough in myself to embrace this next level of healing.

So off I went to a beautiful home clinic where I met Laverne of Chiron Spectra. She's a former senior sales executive who made a life-changing career transition from the cutthroat world of corporate IT to concentrate on her true calling—her passion for energy work.

Her focus is primarily professional women who are looking beyond the surface. Women who are willing to dive deeper to achieve and sustain elevated levels of health and well-being.

Her clients generally fit into one of two categories: the first are going through a spiritual awakening and trying to make sense of it, facing roadblocks around understanding who they are and what they truly value, and looking for a way to move forward. The second are already spiritually awakened and using their spiritual gifts, who are looking to more directly align their life with their soul's purpose. I was clearly in the first category!

There is just so much to know and understand about Transference Healing. I have, with Laverne's blessing, borrowed a few words from her website to help explain this for you.

Transference Healing was channelled and anchored onto the planet by Alexis Cartwright to support the alchemical changes that are naturally occurring with the planet and with each and every one of us. Whilst the human body is naturally going through alchemical changes each day, when you receive a Transference Healing session you are proactively orchestrating this process.

Essentially, the procedures unblock anything that either triggers a genetic weakness (creating a health symptom in the body) OR shows up as limiting your potential to grow and evolve. The process clears stored memory of pain and/or trauma held deep within the body on a subconscious level that may be being experienced in this lifetime as fear or grief.

When Transference Healing® frequency is run you are creating a natural energetic change in the body that purifies distortions which in turn supports a shift. As you make shifts in consciousness you are supporting your awakening process, self-healing (clearing pain, fear, grief) and supporting your ability to self-master.

The procedures accelerate the process of healing that may have otherwise taken years, or even lifetimes to complete. When you work with Transference Healing® you are not only strengthening your direct connection to source, but you also accelerate your ascension process.

The sessions begin with a general conversation, then energy is run through the body to clear blockages, elevating you to a higher level of consciousness, but unconsciously. It's a gentle process where body and spirit dictate how much, and in what areas of life healing occurs. After the procedures were completed, we would have a chat about what came up to be cleared.

Again, this is taken with a level of confidence that the soul knows a hell of a lot more than we consciously do, and our higher self is working with us to come into our most pure and divine incarnation in this lifetime.

A tangible practice Laverne taught me was how to work with nature. Quite a novel concept to begin with, but I soon got the hang of it. The idea is to resource and re-energise by drawing from the natural elements of earth, air, water and fire to regain natural vitality.

So how do I enlist the help of the elements? Well, I simply but deliberately open my awareness, and I ask. I find this is best performed when in nature—on the beach, on a bushwalk, sitting quietly on a rocky outcrop or swimming in the ocean. I ask the energy of nature to replenish my system and resource me. I ask any thoughts, feelings, patterns or stuck toxic energy that no longer serve me to be released and transmuted by nature. I ask for my highest good, and for the highest good for all. I smile, thank the universe and continue with my day. Simple!

Chiron represents the Achilles heel—the core wounding that can stop us from growing and evolving. Feeling our limitations, feeling overwhelmed or feeling frustrated with issues playing out in our lives: that is our Chiron wound playing out. It can manifest through strong emotions, in how we react to situations or as physical symptoms in the body.

The astrological placement of one's Chiron is fundamentally important in Transference Healing. Everyone has a Chiron in their astrological chart, depending on their date of birth. My Chiron is in Aries (the generation born between 1968 and 1977).

The universal message of Chiron is that the key to healing pain is not found outside ourselves, but within. As we heal, we release ourselves from restrictions of the past, transforming and creating a reality of good health, abundance and spiritual freedom. My gift as I overcome my Chiron wounding is empowerment.

I became fascinated with the concept of the Chiron wound, so I went searching for more information. I was fortunate to be guided (thanks, angelic team!) to the wonderful website Astro Butterfly and I appreciate this site articulating the Chiron in Aries wounding so clearly:

Chiron is where we feel wounded, ashamed, broken and inadequate. Chiron in Aries is where you feel you don't have the right to be yourself. Chiron in Aries is about the greatest wound of all— the wound of identity. The wound of identity is when we feel we don't have the right to exist. This is the most painful wound of all because it is the most difficult to grasp.

This wound can play out in several different ways, but I experience it most through the smirks and eye-rolls of those closest to me. People I have opened my heart and soul to, people I have had the courage to confide in, people I deeply care about. I guess if I didn't care about them, my wounds wouldn't be broken open. Perhaps that's the point—only people you care about can truly make you feel.

If the conversation turns to Jason—and I acknowledge that although I may accept that we are not together in this soul incarnation, I may always wonder "what if?" Or when I talk about connecting with my angelic team and trusting their guidance implicitly. Or when I dare dream out loud there could be more to life than living within the perfectly structured boxes society accepts, even demands.

I also feel this judgement when I decline invitations to events when I'm just not up for it. When I embark on overseas adventures like I'm 23 years old again instead of putting the money towards my not-inconsiderable mortgage. Or when I have the audacity to declare that I don't want to live my life the same way as I have lived it up until now.

These judgements and eye-rolls feed my core wound that I am not enough. That I don't deserve to live a life free of fear. That I don't deserve to live a life of love, joy, contentment and bliss. A life in balance. I believe it will be a lifelong process to heal my Chiron wound but acknowledging the wound exists, and that it is multidimensional, is fundamental for the healing to begin.

There was another profound ah-ha moment whilst reading about the Chiron wound. I reflected on how I had spoken to myself for most of my life: "I'm not good enough, I'm not pretty enough, I'm not smart enough." Once again, I was overwhelmed with sadness and tears.

I had to take some (more) time alone to consider what I could do about my feelings of worthlessness. How could I heal such a fundamental wound? I kept reading, knowing in my heart that I was on the right path to understanding this crucial part of myself.

What I learned is that healing this wound was going to be an inside job. No amount of external success, validation or achievements would do it—yet that was how I had been living my life! I had to take responsibility for my own happiness, my own contentment and I had to figure out how to really believe in myself! I had to feel my pain deeply in order to move forward—to be present with my wounds and my shame. It was terrifying. But it is only when the broken parts are recognised, validated and accepted that true healing can occur.

I also recognised that my feelings of unworthiness were manifesting in the infliction of continuous physical wounding to my body—through the overuse of alcohol to numb my existence. To numb the nagging, ever-present feeling that I was not worthy.

It was also manifesting as being a people pleaser—overworking and over-giving in order to receive validation from others, whilst simultaneously invalidating my own needs and desires.

Astro Butterfly then sparked another incredible series of self-directed questions: Could it be that there was a reason that out of billions of genetic combinations, it was ME who made it? Perhaps I do have a right to exist—just as I am—in order to fulfil a unique purpose on the planet at this time.

What if I focused on sharing my gifts and abilities with the world? Could that lead me to inner peace and self-acceptance? Maybe it was time to confront my limiting beliefs and replace them with empowering ones—ones that affirmed my worthiness of a life enlivened with purpose, joy and the most authentic expression of my soul.

Along with the focus of healing the Chiron wound, I identified many other powerful benefits from my Transference Healing sessions. It has allowed me to let go of relationships that were not working with grace, dignity and acceptance. It has allowed me to overcome my considerable frustration that I am not moving forward 'quickly enough'—as if everything isn't in line with divine timing anyway.

Thanks to Transference Healing and my incredible therapist Laverne, I now recognise my higher self is in charge and it doesn't matter what my personality self (my ego) is thinking or telling me, I must surrender to the flow of my life. If I manage to do that, my life will turn out exactly as designed—exactly as my soul intended.

7.
Soul Energy

Meeting Jason lit the spark within me to begin the exploration of my own soul. While diving deeper and deeper into the waters of my quest—guided by my spiritual team—I was introduced to the world of soul connections—soul contracts, soulmates, kindred spirits and twin flames.

As I started learning about these connections, it was tempting to immediately try to fit the people in my life into one of these boxes. Sometimes the box was fairly obvious, but in certain cases it was not. Human reasoning and logic cannot possibly account for the vastness of the universe and the interconnectedness of souls.

Life is messy, the universe is mysterious and we don't get all of our questions answered —that's part of the deal we signed up for. It's one of the many trappings of being human—we want to know all the answers, but what an arrogant thing to demand of this one short and precious lifetime! Looking back I can forgive myself for my eagerness to apply these concepts to every significant relationship I'd ever had, especially Jason.

Soul Contracts

I began my education into all things soulmate related on YouTube mere days after meeting Jason in Margaret River.

I was desperate for knowledge—any information that would provide some level of clarity as to who he was to me and what our connection meant. I spent countless hours listening to lectures and gradually began to grasp a few concepts in the vast world of soul connections.

After I experienced my therapeutic (and traumatic) session with the spiritual healer at Elysia Retreat—where she shared her belief that I had met my twin flame—I went back down the rabbit hole of YouTube in a whole new direction. On her recommendation I started with Matt Kahn's *Soul Contracts, Twin Flames & Soulmates Redefined* lecture. I intuitively felt a resonance with some concepts he shared, particularly when he delved into soul contracts.

A soul contract is a mutual contract between two souls that is predetermined before incarnation in this lifetime. This contract is created so that when two people interact, they energetically pass between each other the information required for their own forward journey. These soul contracts open the possibility for soul growth while we're here on Earth. Of course, once we're here, free will gets a say so there's no guarantee of results, or of soul contracts being completed in any given lifetime.

I don't think we meet people by chance. I believe every significant relationship has been predetermined to maximise a soul's evolution. It may not feel comfortable or beneficial whilst in the experience, but understanding that a higher reason exists has alleviated some of my (self-inflicted) pain and suffering—pain and suffering that, knowing me, would have endured much longer than it needed to.

Once we understand that meeting another soul has been divinely orchestrated we can shift our thinking and ask ourselves more evolved questions. What am I to learn from this person? What am I learning from this *particular encounter* with this person? Is this a recurring theme in my life and if so what lesson am I not integrating? How is this situation or relationship helping me evolve my consciousness? How is it benefiting my soul?

I spent much time considering these questions not only in relation to Jason, but I took the time to reflect on all significant relationships I have experienced in my life. Looking back on old wounds through this new lense brought me feelings of peace, gratitude and, importantly, acceptance of the roles people have played in my evolution.

The idea of pre-incarnation soul contracts required me to take another leap of spiritual faith, but by this time I was happily working with my angelic team, so this leap felt more like a fun little hop. I was also becoming more comfortable trusting the guidance from my higher self, delivered via my oracle readings, and my intuitive hits that always smacked me in the face at the perfect time. I was certainly more open to spiritual concepts than I was prior to my Margaret River experience!

Matt's lecture also focused on what I have come to believe is fundamental—it's how we love, care and respect ourselves that determines whether our life experience is wonderful and fulfilling or excruciating and painful. When we take time to sit with ourselves, when our energy isn't chasing outward but rather is focused inward, when we are consciously open and receptive to beneficial energies, it opens the gateway for our soul's expansion.

Although Matt's lecture was helpful, I still didn't fully understand why the universe had put Jason directly in my path—squarely in my aura—so there was no way I could have avoided our encounter. Nor could I figure out how someone so logical could make the monumental life-changing decisions that I did after such a brief meeting with another soul. My mind couldn't fully comprehend our connection, but perhaps the mind couldn't?

On one level, I was still torturing myself for my failure to bring this relationship into 3D—to the here and now. On another level, I was seeking the greater spiritual meaning of our connection. There had to be one, surely? The universe wasn't so unkind to deliver only heartache, loss and despair—was it?

My imagination ran wild as I agonised over numerous possible soul contracts, created pre-incarnation. Was our agreement that his soul would torture mine in this lifetime? Were the roles reversed in another life where I left him, and it was my soul's turn to be broken into a million pieces? Did I leave him on the docks in England in the

18th century and sail to Australia, never to see him again? Or did I duel him to the death in the Hundred Years War of the 14th century and this was the lifetime for his soul to exact revenge? Heaven, no—please, please, please—is it too late to rewrite those contracts (and have my former incarnations profusely apologise!)?

Soul contracts often carry a lot of emotional energy,
and these intense feelings are meant to propel you forward as
"something" will become too uncomfortable to bear.
A brilliant catalyst for soul growth!
Molly McCord

Not only was I struggling with these pre-determined and mutually agreed soul contract possibilities, but I was also struggling to understand why my wound was still open despite all the work I had done to facilitate my healing. I continued to agonise over innumerable questions. Why couldn't I be *normal* and just let it go? Why was the pain and anguish still hanging around? Why did I struggle to breathe when he entered my consciousness? I'd been able to grieve, accept and then release every relationship that *actually existed* throughout my life, so why was it so hard to let go of the one that didn't?

Soulmates

Having already been introduced to the incredibly insightful and soul-aligned Molly McCord whilst grappling with friendship challenges, my angelic team delivered (via Google) her *Twin Flames Healing Journey* teaching series upon my return from Elysia Retreat. In the introduction, Molly describes the differences in energetic signatures of soulmates, kindred spirits and twin flames. There are 25 lectures in the series, and from the very first lecture I was spellbound.

Molly and I share the belief that soulmates intentionally decide to experience incarnations together. That soulmates are part of a broader soul family. Our soul family often includes family members, lovers, friends, bosses, neighbours and even treasured pets. Soulmates provide the opportunity for mutual soul growth, and movement through the soul's ascension process. None of us experience life on Earth in isolation—what would be the point in that!

There is often an intuitive knowing when someone is connected to us (not necessarily in the relational sense). A feeling, an energetic resonance within, that sparks as soon as they meet. An awareness that may begin a conversation with "Haven't we met before?" or "You seem so familiar to me, I wonder why that is?" Or simply just an easy flow of conversation and a high level of familiarity and comfort together. Soulmate relationships also encompass the full spectrum of human emotions from love, connection, joy and appreciation to fear, resentment, anger and frustration.

I met my dear friend Beck when we were 17 years old. We were both from Australia, but we met as exchange students on the other side of the world. We hit it off immediately. There was a deep connection, an energetic resonance, an intuitive knowing we were meant to connect. We were like twins—even adopting the nicknames Vinnie and Jules from the movie *Twins*, starring Arnold Schwarzenegger and Danny DeVito. Our relationship in Finland was incredibly strong and even though we lived in different parts of the country, we'd find ways to sneak away for a weekend together.

We'd cause mischief in the bars of Turku, with one evening scorched into my memory forever. We were in a crowded bar, celebrating the announcement that Sydney had just been awarded the 2000 Olympics, when my eyes were drawn to a tall, dark and handsome man across the room, surrounded by a group of women. He clocked me at the exact same time and smiled a cheeky smile that made me blush. He left abruptly though, leaving me bitterly disappointed. Ten minutes later, however, having escorted his female friends to another bar, he came back for me. That evening was one of the most memorable of my Finnish experiences. Drop-dead gorgeous 23-year-old *Vogue* model named Larsson—and that's all I'll say about that!

Beck and I also managed to break a few exchange student rules, the rebels that we were. We were on our five-day trip to St Petersburg, Russia. One evening we were invited to a lame underage disco with a group of Russian school students. We took one look at the venue, with a 1960s disco ball hanging from the ceiling and the DJ playing totally uncool music, and devised our escape plan. We snuck out through the fire escape, jumped a cab to the five-star hotel down the road, and enjoyed a steak dinner at the fine-dining restaurant—with our parents' credit cards, of course. There was only so much cabbage and boiled potatoes we could stomach!

We lost contact for quite a few years upon returning to Australia. These were the pre-Facebook and pre-email days (hard to believe there was a time in the world without email, but it's true!). When we found each other again, we organised for our epic reunion to take place in Bali. Our friendship unfolded like no time had passed.

We spent a week enjoying freshly caught fish served on plastic plates at Jimbaran Bay as the sun set over the ocean, sipping on fancy cocktails laced with Finnish vodka whilst watching traditional Balinese dancers perform for the gaggle of tourists, and gossiped into the wee hours of the morning snuggled up in bed together like we were 17 again. It was amazing!

We are soulmates who are completely comfortable being raw and real, deep and meaningful, fun and crazy together. We can speak weekly or a few times a year and it doesn't change the level of affection, closeness or connection we share. I treasure my relationship with my Vinnie!

Alas, not every soulmate is a Vinnie, and several experiences spring to mind (mainly with the opposite sex). If someone is not treating me well, not respecting me, will I honour myself and take back my power? Will I sever the connection—as enticing and seductive as someone might be—to demonstrate self-respect and self-love?

After everything I've learned I certainly feel better equipped to embrace soul growth and embody self-love. Sure, there will continue to be connections that challenge or frustrate me, even devastate me, but after making it this far I know I can handle anything (or anyone) the universe decides to throw at me. Whoever is meant for me will find me, and I'll be ready to embrace them with open arms and an open heart.

I also learnt from Molly that soulmates are often working on the same healing themes in a given lifetime, such as betrayal, abandonment, receptivity to love or self-worth. After reflecting on common themes within my family, I have a clearer understanding of the healing we are working through together in this incarnation. In particular I have come to realise that the wound of unworthiness has been passed down through multiple generations.

As I considered the lack of self-esteem many of my family members have struggled with in this lifetime, the newly embodied knowledge of my Chiron wound came flooding back. It took my breath away and although it made me sad, I was simultaneously exhilarated as the puzzle pieces connected in my soul. Yes! Achievement unlocked! Gratitude washed over me as I integrated another layer of understanding and acceptance that our stories are much bigger than any one lifetime.

The universe, through multiple interactions both within the family and with other souls, is continually affirming that self-love and self-acceptance—just as I am—is of fundamental importance for my soul's ascension. I am now aware and committed to healing this wound for the benefit of this life experience, and other incarnations on the non-linear timeline of my soul.

Soulmates are often our greatest teachers. The circles of karma though are always spinning, and we may play different roles in different lifetimes in order to experience growth and healing from different angles. I am my daughters' mother in this incarnation, but our roles could be reversed in the next. I introduced this concept to my youngest daughter over dinner one evening, and she emphatically declared that she is coming back as my mother—to make sure I eat all my broccoli!

Although soulmates may trigger us the most, they can also be our greatest gifts—if we can observe and assess the relationship from a higher perspective, which isn't always easy! I considered Jason in this context—he certainly brought out the full spectrum of emotions in me. He certainly triggered me in a way no other soul has (thus far) in this lifetime. Was he my greatest gift? I believe only time (and potentially the reckoning when I cross over from this lifetime) will tell.

In this lifetime, we are connecting with unfinished stories that are asking us for an energetic resolution. You will recognise these fellow soul travellers through your deep emotional reactions to them. Your soul story with them is much bigger than this lifetime, or perhaps any one lifetime
Molly McCord

In the meantime, I'll do my best to stay open and receptive, and delight in the anticipation of whoever comes along next. I'll also remind myself as often as I need to that soulmate love is never lost—it simply changes form each incarnation.

Kindred Spirits

A kindred spirit has a different energetic signature to a soulmate. Soul recognition is present but we come in without all the karmic wounds and lessons to work through together. Emotional turmoil is *nearly* non-existent with kindred spirits; instead, there is peaceful, loving energy that feels like it's existed across many lifetimes. The connection is based in pure heart energy.

The kindred spirits in my life are the ones who just *get* me—we are on the same frequency. In a group conversation where an *interesting* perspective is being shared, a kindred spirit will already know what I'm thinking because they are thinking the very same thing. It's telepathic! We exchange a knowing glance or a sly smile and revel, happily, in our shared understanding and connection.

Charmayne is a kindred spirit of mine. We met at boarding school at 15 years of age, and although not initially close, that changed when we miraculously (thank you, universe!) bumped into each other in a coffee shop in Sydney—a city of over five million people—eight years later.

We have been by each other's side since then, sharing wholeheartedly in life's challenges and joys and heartache and turmoil. She knows me better than I know myself. We have never had a fight, and we seldom disagree. If we do, there is patience and kindness and never any judgement. What an incredible blessing!

Kindred spirits, being like-minded and like-souled people with whom an instant connection of love and understanding is mutually experienced, can appear at any moment. The universe will orchestrate the introduction when it's the right time for both to support each other through the next level of healing and growth.

I was sitting at home one day feeling lonely and melancholy, reflecting on the friends (and relationships) that had left my sphere since my awakening began. If I'm honest, I was feeling more than a little sorry for myself. In that moment, however, instead of continuing to wallow in the negative emotions, I consciously and determinedly switched up the energy.

I audaciously declared to the universe that it was the right time to bring in another aligned soul for the next chapter of my life. Another soul who would just *get* me—where I didn't need to explain my spirituality or defend my beliefs. I sent my request into the heavens, smiled, and said thank you, understanding that all I had to do was be open and receptive.

I then immediately laughed out loud to myself, recognising my insanely implausible request. "Amanda, you have to actually leave your apartment in order to meet someone new!" I shook my head and continued to laugh, recognising the universe was highly unlikely to deliver my new kindred spirit to my front door in my secure complex!

A week later I was lying by the communal pool, working on my suntan and watching the kids swim, squeal and divebomb with their friends. The gate opened and a woman I had never laid eyes on before walked in with a beaming smile on her face. She introduced herself as Nicole, who had just moved from New York. Voila: hello there, kindred spirit!

Nicole and I became fast friends, immediately recognising our deep soul connection. She invited me to a Goddess ceremony at the local yoga studio, later confiding she already knew, the moment we met, that I would say yes. She recognised me before I did her! Since that day by the pool, we have been inseparable.

Our activities range from full-moon rituals conducted on my balcony, to saluting the sun in my living room, to engaging in deep and honest conversations about ... well, everything! We have an intuitive sense we lived together in 18th century England. We both strongly identify with Jane Austen, sharing a mutual affection for the tall, dark and handsome Mr Darcy. Our affection (okay, lust) for Colin Firth's portrayal is evidence of that! We have shimmers of memories from those incarnations: rolling green hills, high tea in suspiciously similar stone courtyards, and shedding our stifling corsets for a skinny-dip in a tranquil swimming hole when we knew we wouldn't be caught!

Importantly, we can also hold each other accountable—even when difficult truths need to be shared, or potentially controversial opinions expressed (or let's face it—when she gently assures me that someone in my life isn't good for me and it's time to let them go!). It's so fascinating—the messages always land just as intended, in our cocoon of safety, trust and genuine love for one another. She's an incredible cheerleader, co-conspirator and soul sister. I am so excited to have a new playmate in my life!

Twin Flames

Molly's teaching series—unsurprisingly—focuses on the twin flame connection. My appetite for this knowledge was insatiable, and the expansion of my consciousness—the broadening and deepening of my understanding of soul connections—was nothing short of revolutionary. This work introduced a possible alternative soul relationship with Jason. If I'm honest, most lectures were traumatic and heartbreaking.

Twin flame energy is closely related to soulmate energy but with a few key differences. We all have many soulmates (and kindred spirits) that appear throughout our lives; however, we only have one twin flame. When we first encounter our twin, there is an intense sense of attraction, recognition and longing—a feeling of finally coming home. I lost my breath when I first heard Molly's words.

I was immediately transported to the long grasses and olive trees of the West Australian bushland. I again felt his lips on mine where our energies connected and our souls merged. Where, when we broke apart, the very first words he uttered were, "Oh no." I felt calm and simultaneously overwhelmed. I felt molecular expansion in my heart. I felt a heavenly peace in my body and soul. It was the most unforgettable moment of my life.

There was an undeniable *knowing* that we had been brought together by a higher power. It activated and expanded—even more—within me. More than I had ever considered possible. The twin flame connection is considered to be the most powerful soul connection a person can experience. There also exists an *unbreakable* energetic cord of attachment between twins. This newly unearthed information challenged all my logical and mental understandings of our vast universe, and the energies that dwell within it.

I remember lying in my sauna listening to the lectures with tears streaming down my face and my body convulsing uncontrollably. If I could have rolled myself into a tight ball in the confined space, I definitely would have done so. My instinct to crunch myself into the foetal position was overwhelming—it was the only way I could think to protect myself as I buckled under the weight of Molly's words.

There is a belief in some circles that a twin flame 'completes' you, but I don't entirely agree. It is my belief that a twin flame, through the devastation of not being together, encourages you to complete yourself in your own time, in your own power. Through meeting them you are challenged to become the person you are meant to become in this lifetime.

Twinflames
You only have one twin flame.
One soul that can bring you back
to your true authentic self.
One soul who truly loves every part of you.
You are eternally connected
and unlike other connections,
it's the only love that can never be
eroded by time or difficulties
Amanda Hicks

Sometimes called a 'mirror soul', our twin is considered to be our other half. The idea is that one soul gets split into two bodies—akin to human twins developing from the splitting of one embryo. Twins have parallel growth paths, and come to Earth with the same karma, soul wounds and lessons to learn in this lifetime. The connection is both challenging and healing, reflecting our deepest insecurities, fears and shadows but also revealing to us our greatest strengths.

Although this information initially induced another jolt of despair, my logical mind quickly re-engaged. I recognised, matter-of-factly, that I could not confirm any of this. It had been ten months since we met and we had not spoken a single word to each other.

I had to be completely, and brutally, honest with myself. I didn't actually know much about him at all—his upbringing, his parents or siblings, or his life experiences. I didn't know what soul wounds he was working through (consciously or unconsciously), and I didn't know what life path he was on. For someone so accustomed to ticking defined boxes, it was torturous not being able to pick up my pen, decisively mark the correct box, and consider the case closed.

Regardless of the label I wanted to assign to him, Jason's rejection and abandonment of our connection was what forced me to find the strength and bravery to begin the healing of myself, all by myself. The journey has taken me to the deepest and darkest parts of my soul. I recognised though, there was no other choice, except death. And I had so, so, so much to live for.

I also learnt that twins' life experiences can be lived at different speeds, so they may not come together in any given lifetime and complete the work. Tragically, when one twin doesn't want to move forward in the connection, it triggers an inevitable chain reaction—igniting the other twin's core wounds again—this time in *full consciousness*. The expression 'dark night of the soul' was introduced into my vocabulary. The magnificent power of this assertion reverberated through my body and soul.

If twin flames do come back together—if they've both done the inner healing work mandated by this connection—there is celebration on an infinitely deep level. This is a soul connection of unconditional love, transcending space and time. Sounds like heaven on earth to me.

Even with all the knowledge I had assimilated about soul energies, I found it excruciating coming to terms with the fact Jason wouldn't be mine to move forward with. But I had to honour that I am not the only one in the connection. There are two of us, and we both have free will. He exercised his and I had to be okay with his decision. I *have* to be okay with his decision.

Soul Alignment

I was listening to a podcast on Spotify on the walk to work one morning. It was Caitlyn Pasternak's *Sexy Soul Radio*. She is a feisty, progressive and charismatic woman who uses her podcast to delve into all things soul related. She's fun to listen to, sure, but has a way of communicating some pretty serious messages regarding soul growth too.

One episode really struck me and I decided to do more research. She interviewed Christopher Power on the concept of Human Design. I had never heard about it, but the interview was fascinating and my intuition was setting off alarm bells—letting me know to pay attention. I didn't listen to this particular interview, on this particular podcast, on this particular day, at this particular time on my soul's evolution *not* to take notice. So, I booked a session with Christopher and I'll be forever grateful that I did.

I spent the first 20 minutes talking about me, which of course included Jason and the subsequent changes I had made to my life. I hadn't made a conscious decision to give him such an extensive overview prior to our appointment, and it was certainly uncharacteristic for me to let down my guard and be so revealing, but he radiated such calm, soothing energy that I just ... did.

On reflection I believe it was because he was an Australian who understood the Australian psyche and therefore, by extension, me.

He later informed me that he never lets clients talk for that long, and certainly not without interruption. He usually jumps right in, commandeering the consultation with little initial input. But having taken a look at my human design chart he immediately knew to just stay quiet.

Once I was finished, he gave me a comparatively brief synopsis of how human design works: Human design is part science, part mysticism and part spirituality. It combines the teachings of astrology, I-Ching, Kabbalah, the chakra system and quantum physics. It reveals to us our uniqueness as sovereign beings. Our human design chart is the roadmap back to our authentic self.

We arrive on Earth with unique gifts and innate wisdom, but we are bombarded with innumerable and persistent outside influences that are trying to convince us who we are *supposed* to be in order to 'fit in' or 'make it' in this life. That all sounded terribly familiar to me.

There were many insights I was, at best, only partially conscious of. I guess that was the point. I was being introduced to my *unconscious* characteristics and not just the aspects of self I had already met!

Understanding my human design allowed me to appreciate the journey I was on and understand that it was, in fact, divinely in line with my soul's plan. That revelation alone was worth the price of the consultation. It also allowed me to begin the process of forgiving myself for the pain I caused those dearest to me after meeting Jason.

The first point Christopher made, he made very early, very clearly and very deliberately. "Listen carefully to me, Amanda. Jason was a gift from the universe. He was your catalyst. He woke you up." I attracted him at the exact time he was required for my soul's evolution. And he did his job brilliantly. Just brilliantly. He didn't stay, because he was never meant to.

The second deliberate point was that I was exactly where I was meant to be. He acknowledged it was incredibly intense but was right on time for what I was meant to experience and how I was meant to grow and evolve. "You are here to make things happen."

He asked me, "If you got what you wanted, what would it be?

What would it look like?" It was rhetorical, an invitation for me to really consider what it was I *actually* wanted. On reflection, I find it almost incredulous (and embarrassing to admit) that I hadn't thought about setting intentions for what I wanted my life to look like in totality. I had tended to focus on one or two specific aspects—relationships, children, financial security, my next holiday, friendships, career progression or physical health. I hadn't taken the time to create a holistic view of my life on this planet.

I certainly hadn't thought about how I would like to feel in my life. *Feel?* What's that but a fleeting sensation within a moment in time? Who has the time to consider how they want to feel? I have to DO, DO, DO! Well, it appeared that things were starting to come together, building on what I had discovered in my kinesiology sessions.

Could it be that I wasn't meant to run through life at 100 miles per hour? Wasn't meant to have a to-do list pages long, thwarting any possible opportunity to just sit and breathe? Was it possible, just *possible,* that I wasn't meant to *do* all the *doing* all the time? That I wasn't meant to sacrifice my well-being to ensure everyone else was looked after?

My internal dialogue then took a surprising detour: Do I deserve love just as I am, without having to achieve or prove anything to earn it? From myself and from others? Am I enough in this world just being Amanda?

Christopher continued, explaining the only way I could move forward was to work on myself to ensure this lifetime fulfills its potential. The doer in me immediately panicked—where would I possibly find the time? How could I be so *selfish?* My mind swirled with all of the people and projects that would *surely* suffer if I dared to take some time for myself. My inner child—often ignored and rejected—*knew* this information was vital to the awakening of my soul and suddenly screamed at me to listen! I took some deep breaths and focused on calming my nervous system so that I could at least *consider* his guidance.

Christopher affirmed that I had gone as far as possible on the traditional career-marriage-house-children trajectory and that self-development must become my primary focus for a period of time. He declared—really to ensure I was listening—that if I took the time to focus on *my* self and on *my* growth, my children, ex-husband, family, friends, co-workers and clients would all get to receive and experience the person they were meant to—authentic Amanda. I exhaled. Neither of us spoke for a full minute.

After giving me time to integrate these incredibly accurate and insightful messages, Christopher asked if I was okay to continue. I assured him that I was wholeheartedly ready to keep peeling back the layers of Amanda!

In my human design chart, I have many open centres, meaning I can be influenced in both very positive and very negative ways. In particular, I need to be selective about my physical environment as it sets me up for either success or bitterness (these are the key indicators of whether a Projector in Human Design—me—is on or off track). When choosing if physical spaces are right for me, I need to ask these questions: Is there positive energy around? Are the people around me alive and vibrant? Are they coming from a good place in their heart? And then—and this is the harder part—I have to actually tune in to my instinctive knowing.

If the answer is positive, fantastic! If it is negative, I will absorb the toxic energy into my body and flounder. No wonder the city of Sydney, with the ongoing construction and a million people pulsing with their energies (certainly not all positive), put me on edge. My professional environment of the past 20 years was not aligned with my physical, mental and soul's need for calm. The city was seriously depleting my already overtaxed nervous system. It was purely my defined willpower centre (okay, and a bit of stubbornness) that allowed me to persist for so many years.

The next helpful insight—laughter is the *best* medicine for me. When I am worrying or criticising myself or being too logical, my body needs laughter. This also relates to my Scorpionic nature. My intensity gets distorted when I'm consumed by logical thinking and I become far too serious. When I break the cycle with laughter my intensity ebbs and logic gets a break.

Anyone who can help me surrender to life in the present moment by eliciting a hearty belly chuckle is hugely resourcing for my system. It's why I enjoy movies (especially romantic comedies), stand-up comedy shows and anyone who can tell a great joke. My ex-husband first drew me in with his fabulous sense of humour. It was all beginning to make more sense. The pieces of the Amanda puzzle were clicking, slowly but surely, into place.

Another revelation that had me cheering on the inside was the confirmation that my body needs excess pampering! This explained my constant desire for massage, facials and healing therapies. Turns out, these rituals are highly supportive for my system. It's funny, I have friends who can take or leave a massage, facial, body treatment, etc. I could never understand that mindset as I can never experience enough!

I asked a question about alcohol, and in particular, my overindulgence with wine. I confided that when I am out of balance, stressed or grumpy, I don't seem to have an off switch. He considered my chart, and immediately honed in on my pressurised, and completely open root centre. He explained that any external energy I receive from others is amplified, so if my friend wants another glass of wine, I will feed off that energy, immediately agree and very often up the ante: "Absolutely, but let's get a bottle instead of a glass!" My defined willpower doesn't stand a chance.

He offered the following advice. When the craving for alcohol hits, I have to make the craving work for *me*. Instead of reaching for the glass to numb my pain or reduce my intensity, turn my attention inward and explore what is *really* going on in my life. Where is the pain, what am I not seeing, what am I not assimilating? Take time to sit in self-reflection. Then make decisive moves towards alternative sources of pleasure—laughter, sex with someone I love, a romantic comedy or disco diva concert!

I am learning through (much) trial and (much) error that when I am in balance, I can have two to three glasses of wine and receive genuine pleasure. I can then say no thank you to another glass. I can respect my body and my desire to experience a happy and healthy following day without a hangover. Nowadays—and no one is more surprised about this than I am—I often make the decision to say no thank you to the first glass!

Christopher concluded the consultation elegantly: "Amanda, you are learning how to deal with intense emotions—or put another way—how to be intensely emotional, authentic, transformed and independent in a way that is conscious, a way that is real."

An hour after our consultation, I was sitting at my kitchen table, enjoying a glass of iced lemon water, and reflecting in silence. The threads of everything I had experienced over the last year and a half were weaving together in my mind, in my heart and in my soul. I had been energetically attracting people, experiences and situations (and podcasts!) to assist my soul's evolution. And I wasn't doing it alone—I was being guided and supported every step of the way by Spirit.

My discovery of human design has facilitated a deeper level of understanding and acceptance of myself. I want to be a woman who knows her power authentically but doesn't need to bulldoze other people to prove it. I want to transform in this lifetime and return to my soul—unapologetically as myself. I want to sit in *my* authenticity, *my* truth, *my* pure power.

It's time for the phoenix to rise.

8.
A New Dawn

I am the love I have been seeking ...

I am home.

A new dawn was breaking, a new year was beginning—and it showed much promise.

I celebrated New Year's Eve with Jackie at a fabulous Japanese restaurant, woke up without a screaming hangover and enjoyed a beautiful New Year's Day on the beach where the surf was cool and inviting. As I lay on my beach towel, I welcomed the sense of renewed optimism for my life. I was open to new possibilities, open to working with and receiving benevolent universal energy, open to new people and experiences.

I reflected on how dramatically my world had changed since meeting Jason. I was (mostly) very proud of the way I had navigated the tumultuous waters and was looking forward to my future. I was raring to go, and I was confident it would be my best year in many.

My gorgeous girls were happy and settled. They moved easily and frictionlessly between their parents on a week-on, week-off basis. There were never any troubles at handover, just a "See ya, Mum, See ya, Dad," after enjoying a family dinner together. The smooth transition from a one-house household to a two-house arrangement is testament to the way Brad and I have navigated the changing nature of our relationship. Our separation and divorce has been, frankly, a resounding success and I earnestly thank him for the way he accepted and moved through the changes and challenges inflicted on his life.

We are a team for our precious children and my dear wish is that although we don't enjoy a traditional family home life, they understand both parents love and support them. We are their biggest cheerleaders in life.

As a mother, I now know that my primary role is to encourage my children to discover and rejoice in their uniqueness, and not deny their gifts and talents just to fit in. To guide my children to celebrate their individuality and accept themselves wholeheartedly, without apology. They are perfect, just as they are.

I also considered my role as a daughter. I want to be the daughter who not only succeeds as dictated by the society in which we live but I argue, more importantly, who finally breaks free and claims who she was all along. A gift I now recognise I would be eternally grateful to receive as a mother.

I also reflected on the multi-generational cycle of low self-worth. Severing this cord and breaking these chains, not only for myself but for my gorgeous daughters, is crucial. The only way I can do that is to continue to respect, honour and engage in the elevation of my own worth as a healthy, happy and thriving woman. I want to be a woman who contributes to society from a place of authentic power, in a service capacity, for the benefit of other souls on the planet.

My health was much improved thanks to a balance of morning walks on the beach to welcome the day (summer, not winter—I'm a bit of a rise-with-the-sun girl), weekend hikes exploring the incredible natural scenery on my doorstep (thanks, Patagonia!), yoga classes for strength and stretch (not to mention the calm and meditative qualities yoga bestows), and fitness classes for cardio which also ensured my escape from the office at lunchtime (ballet barre is my favourite!). Gone were the long lunches and the excessive drinking—my health was now a top priority.

As I entered the new year I was fit, healthy and feeling more physically attractive than I had in many years. I still wasn't exactly where I wanted to be, but I was happy and content and could approach the world with my shoulders back, head held high and a beaming smile on my face.

My relationships with some friends had changed but I had made peace with my altered friendship landscape. Some connections had faded into the background or even left my sphere since my separation, but I recognised and accepted this was part of the journey through life. Where the magic and wonder burst through was in the authentic and honest relationships I had cultivated with existing and new friends. I had developed such a richness of connection with certain souls and I felt incredibly blessed.

I want to be that friend who can not only enjoy giggles, adventures and the occasional cocktail lying by a pool in an exotic destination, but also hold space for critical discussions on heartache, despair, loss, trauma, grief and disappointment. Friendships that embrace all the characteristics and emotions of the soul are worth their weight in gold.

I was even able to be at peace with the men who had come and gone from my world. There was growth and healing to be experienced and enjoyed, even if it took me a little longer than most to appreciate the reasons and lessons for them being in (and out) of my life. I was happy staying out of the dating game, content to focus on going inward and learning about myself. I now understood the universe was working with me, always in my highest good, and the right soul would magically appear—in divine timing—when we were both ready. I was happy to wait.

Work was still intense, but I was thriving, thanks to my new health regimen and optimistic outlook, and the self-worth and confidence that gave me—well, I lapped it up. I had just strung together two very positive (thus, financially lucrative) years and was feeling confident in my ability to continue to succeed in my career. In particular, I enjoyed being part of a successful, productive and engaged corporate team. They certainly became true friends and confidants as I navigated the ever-changing landscape that was my life, tolerating and supporting the many faces of Amanda throughout that time!

I had, though, begun to question if the world of financial services, with the early morning travel, ever-increasing corporate demands and the physical work environment of the CBD were in alignment with my true soul path. There were many aspects of my role that I enjoyed, namely interacting with my clients and being of service to them, but I began to wonder: could I be of service to souls in another way?

Perhaps I was being introduced to the infinite vastness of the universe, my spiritual team and human design for a reason? Perhaps my own personal transformation was part of a larger story? Perhaps these breadcrumbs were being deliberately dropped to course correct a life that was not fulfilling its true purpose? I took the first step and enrolled, part time, in the study of both reinvention coaching and BG5. The rest, as they say, is history.

As I left the beach that day I felt at peace with myself and enthusiastic for the next chapter of my life that was, in reality, just beginning. There was only one more occasion I had to face ...

The Anniversary

Two years to the day I met Jason.
I knew it was approaching. I could feel it in my body. I could sense it in my soul. My anxiety was rising, and my mind had taken me back to that clear but brisk morning in the gorgeous Western Australian bushland a few times over the last few weeks.

From my journal:

> *Today is the day—two years on from when I was turned upside down, inside out and spun around so fast I questioned if it even happened. But it did. And it changed my life forever.*

To add to the energetic impact, the anniversary fell during an intense full moon. I was tired and on edge at the same time. The children had been challenging and I had raised my voice a few too many times in recent days. There was structural building work happening in my apartment so my usually comforting and safe space wasn't safe. I was forced to seek alternative accommodations.

I really needed to be alone. I needed Amanda time. I needed spiritual guidance. So I grounded myself and conducted a reading to celebrate the anniversary. In truth, I never imagined spending the second anniversary of meeting Jason not blissfully embraced in his arms.

I breathed deeply, felt into my heart and picked up my Wisdom of the Oracle deck. Before I even began to shuffle, my intuition nudged me to look at the card at the bottom of the deck. Something I very rarely do. But I trusted my intuition and my guides implicitly. I turned the card over and lost my breath. It was *Soul Mates*. Of course it was.

I understand that now. I understand the soul connection I share with Jason well. I hadn't noticed until then (unbelievable, but true) it is card number 41. I was 41 years of age when I met him.

I looked at the imagery. It was gorgeous. It was perfect. It was aligned. I laughed out loud. It was yet another ah-ha moment on my journey. It was us.

Two penguins—the male holding a golden key, the female with a keyhole at her heart's centre. They are resting their heads on each other with a flurry of bright red love hearts swirling around. Spirit is looking lovingly down upon them both.

It completely mirrored the way we sat that morning amongst the tall grasses of the Western Australian bushland—side by side with my head resting on his shoulder, his head resting on mine. Our hands and hearts intertwined. Our breath connected. I felt the way I did that morning two years earlier—content, fulfilled, peaceful, soul-connected, in love.

SOUL MATES

Essential meanings: Harmonious partnerships; love; friendship; companionship; a relationship fostering personal growth.

"Certain people enter into your life in order to take you to the next level of healing, consciousness, and authenticity." Nothing to add—the message was clear. This is my return to self, return to authenticity, return to love healing journey—I believe the most important of my lifetime.

"You know these people by the strong pull drawing you towards them." Absolutely. There was a magnetic, universal force drawing the two of us together that evening, and we were powerless in the energy. I certainly was: There was nothing I could do, no other reaction was possible—regardless of my logical mind. I could not resist. I could not turn away. This was my pre-determined soul contracted path. This was my destiny. *He* was my destiny.

"Soul mates can be friends for life or remain in your life for only a short time." Well, I think I may have set the record here!

"No matter what, you will be changed in ways you can't possibly fathom now. Pay attention to these people today. They are your

greatest gifts." Again, no ambiguity here. My life has changed in so, so, so many ways. I certainly could not have ever comprehended this one encounter, in the most unexpected of circumstances and locations, could change my life in such a significant and dramatic way.

From the Relationship message of *Soul Mates*: "*Consider love in the deepest sense—love so powerful that you will never be the same, regardless of how long your relationship lasts. Consider friendships and romantic bonds so compelling that they overwhelm you with gratitude ... or break you open so you will finally claim who you were meant to be.*"

Reading the message brings me to tears, even now. Every single message held within the Oracle resonates with me so deeply. There is no doubt in my mind, in my heart or in my soul Jason is a soulmate of mine. He has chosen another path and that is his choice. He has free will, and I honour that. I honour him.

> *Jason,*
>
> *Meeting you changed my life and although it has undoubtedly been a traumatic, emotional, physical and especially spiritual journey, it has been worth it.*
>
> *To stand where I do now—in my power, in my body, in my spirit and with unwavering belief in myself—that is your gift to me.*
>
> *I wish for you love, success and of course, an authentic and meaningful connection with another soul.*
>
> *Amanda x*

In gratitude, there is no grief.

A few hours after the reading which was cathartic but still heartbreaking and laced with the sadness of what could have been, I asked myself the question: "How am I?"

Well, as I sit here on a glorious, clear, blue and unseasonably warm day in Sydney, I check in. I *really* check in. To my mind. To my heart. And of course, to my soul. I am okay.

Actually, I am more than okay ...

I am here, as I am arriving
I am known, as I am knowing
I am understanding the truth of who I am
I am emerging
I am meeting and I am merging
with the ocean of oneness within
I am the love I have been seeking
I am home.

Epilogue

A Word from Charmayne

Amanda is a very successful career woman who has a high level of respect in her industry working for one of the largest financial services companies in the world. She's achieved all this in a sales capacity when she's actually an introvert and prefers time by herself and not in the hustle of one of the most demanding industries in the world. That demonstrates her incredible strength and tenacity. Her incredible willpower.

She has always been the social hostess with the mostess—hosting dozens of friends for BBQs and pool parties that would start at midday and often not end until way after the sun had gone down. She and Brad always catered amazingly—ensuring everyone was well satisfied and had a fabulous time. We always knew it was going to be an 'event' when the invitation arrived.

Her health and fitness were variable though—she could never quite manage to stay consistently fit and this area of life was always a struggle for her. She could be persuaded for lunch over the gym most days so her focus wasn't truly on her own well-being. She indulged in the wines too often, as most of us did, but didn't back up in the way most of us could so suffered terribly with hangovers and all the negativity and self-loathing that came with that.

Her relationship with her husband from the outside looked more than just okay. They were a lovely couple who were great partners and wonderful parents to their girls.

She managed her divorce in the most amazing way I could ever have imagined, and am unlikely to see again. They are still friends who see each other for dinners, holidays, and all school and social activities. They are still a team, a partnership focused on the health and well-being of their children. It's incredibly rare to see this type of divorce but if anyone were going to achieve it, it would be Amanda.

She did make some questionable choices with the men in her life over the last few years—some she dragged in and some came for her. But I recognise the lessons she learned and these experiences have ultimately been beneficial for her growth. There was no point telling her not to see or contact or be with someone anyway—she was determined to have these experiences without anyone's counsel.

But I had never seen her in distress, real 'she might not make it through this' distress. Until Jason. I was the first she told—as soon as she was back from the trip—and I knew immediately she had changed. She was certain he was her soulmate and they would be together.

As the months dragged on without a word from him, I became really worried. She began to withdraw more from our social circle and spent more time alone. Her drinking increased and her sense of vibrancy faded fast. I wasn't sure if she would make it through the experience of meeting him. I had never seen anything like it. I tried valiantly to understand it, but it was just so, so deep—I couldn't meet her there.

I am so glad Jason didn't come for her, or she wouldn't be the person she is today. She wouldn't have had to go 'in' and do the incredibly difficult work she's done over the last few years to really become her true self. To become the woman she's meant to be. Had he appeared as she so desperately wanted (and for some time couldn't believe it wasn't going to happen) she wouldn't have grown or evolved like she has.

Thank you, Jason, for not coming back. You've been the greatest gift to her. Now she is strong and smart and capable and truly knows herself, loves herself and is her greatest advocate.

Look out universe—if you thought she was successful before,

just wait to see what she can do when she's really in her power. When she's really in her truth.

I, for one, will be with her every step of the way, as her second greatest cheerleader.

Thank-Yous

This book would not have been possible without the input and support of so many people.

First, my gorgeous daughters - Grace and Lauren:

From the moment you both came into the world, you have given me indescribable joy and pleasure. I love watching you grow and evolve into happy, healthy and independent humans with a zest and sparkle for life.

You really were **the** reason I found the strength to just keep going. There is no greater gift I could ever have received.

I am so proud of you both. I make you both this promise: I will be there for you every step of the way on your journeys. I will continue to do my best to guide, educate and comfort you through the challenges that life will throw your way.

I love you both with all my heart, to the moon and back. xx

My parents - Tom and Robyn:

The support I have enjoyed from you both has been crucial to enabling me to continue my new life's path, as uncertain (even terrifying) as it has been at times. I won the universal lottery at birth, and I am incredibly grateful for you both.

Thank you for your constant support of not just me, but Grace and Lauren who love and adore you to bits. I love you both so much.

My ex-husband - Brad:

·I extend a heartfelt thank you for your acceptance and support of our new life circumstances, knowing full well you would never have chosen this yourself. Your ongoing support of me, and our precious girls has been beyond compare.

I am so lucky to have you in my life as my friend, and as the wonderful, caring and kind father you are. My wish is that we can continue to work together for the benefit of our daughters, regardless of who comes (or goes) from our lives in the future.

My closest friends -
Charmayne, Nicole, Krystyna, Jackie, Alex,
Beck and Tess:

A heartfelt thank you for your continued friendship over the last few years. I love having you all in my life and I cherish the ability to learn from you, enjoy hearty belly-laughs, and indulge in incredible experiences together. Authentic friendships at their finest.

A special thank you to Nicole for helping me navigate the Covid crisis in our incredible complex, and Beck who became my legal counsel - the rockstar lawyer to the stars that you are!

My unofficial editorial team - Charmayne, Steph, Nicole and Nancy:

My deep appreciation to **Charmayne**, as when I recognised my story may not just be for my own healing and growth, she encouraged me to carefully craft the essence of the story for wider consumption. Thank you, Char!

My friend **Steph**, being an expert marketer, immediately recognised what I hadn't - the independent chapters were broader themes, and if grouped correctly, I could guide the reader from basic healing themes through the complexity of soul energies. She was right! Thank you, Steph!

My kindred spirit **Nicole** didn't enter my life until the book was 'complete'. It was so valuable to have a soul-sister provide an independent editorial perspective (having not lived the experience with me). Her profound spiritual knowledge guided me, and ensured I articulated concepts clearly. She also assured me that I would provide comfort and guidance to others on their healing journey, giving me the confidence to seek a publisher. Thank you, Nicole!

My amazing mentor **Nancy Pickard** offered to read this as an early draft and I jumped at the chance to receive guidance from the global best-selling author of 'Bigger, Better, Braver' and master life-coach! Her key advice was invaluable. Thank you Nancy!

My professional, independent editor - Chelsea Rider-Robinson:

Chelsea was a gift from the universe. We collaborated on every theme, anecdote, and word choice. She coaxed more details out of me which elevated the reading experience (and me well out of my comfort zone). I grew into a writer during our time, and I am grateful our paths crossed. Thank you, Chelsea!

My energy health care professionals - Ghislaine and Laverne:

I am so fortunate to have had the opportunity to work with Ghislaine. Her kindness, patience and guidance has been beyond compare, and I thank you, Ghislaine, from the bottom of my heart.

Laverne opened my eyes to the energy outside the realms of the physical body, and the connection she facilitated between my earthly form and my higher self has absolutely expedited my healing. Thank you so much!

The men who helped me - Jason, Aiden, Luke and Tim:

We don't meet people by accident. We meet people at the perfect time to teach us about life, love and most importantly how to learn, grow, and heal. My story with each of you is unique and I accept that each experience was divinely guided. I wish for you all a happy, healthy and abundant life. Thank you for being part of my journey.

The incredible astrologer - Molly McCord:

Since discovering Molly's work, I have become a stronger, more aligned and more appreciative human. Her understanding of astrology, intuitive guidance and genuine authenticity that oozes through every podcast and online course has made (and continues to make) an incredible contribution to my spiritual evolution. Thank you, Molly!

My Oracle Card Goddess - Colette Baron-Reid:

The discovery of your work has been instrumental in guiding me through the most challenging and confronting of situations. I continue to rely on your wisdom, and don't know where I'd be without my oracle cards! Thank you, Colette!

My musical saviour - Diana Ross:

Diana, my heart belongs to you and the incredible talented songwriters Nile Rodgers and Bernard Edwards for THE song that kept me going when all hope had left my body. For all the times I didn't feel I would make it through this experience, *I'm Coming Out* lifted me out of my despair long enough to take one more step. My heartfelt thank you!

My coaching mentor - Nancy Levin:

Nancy, your thoughtful and instinctive guidance through LLCA has been instrumental in developing my skills as a Reinvention coach. I love the passion you have for the art and science of coaching and am grateful for your personal guidance and professional knowledge. Thank you, Nancy!

My work family - Sav, Steph, Wendy, Andy and Matt:

I was lucky enough to have a second family I could lean on for support and who rode the full ride of ups and downs by my side. Thank you for tolerating and supporting me throughout that time! I am so blessed to still consider you my friends. Thank you!

The 'PC Crew':

I was fortunate to secure a wonderful home post separation and have been blessed with an awesome community. A shout out to Nicole, Chris, Indi and Darcy; Pete, Golasa, Oscar and Avery; Lisa, Ben, Kyra, Caitlin and Zavier; Nicky, Antony and Penelope; Becs, Steve, Ivy and Ellysia; and Caroline, Gary, Eva, Camille and Charlie.

My Flashpack crew - Argentina:

Thank you friends for the conversations that enriched and nourished me. Perhaps you didn't realise it at the time, but the adventure we shared helped me heal another level of discord within me.

My Flashpack crew - Morocco:

My Morocco adventure didn't make the final edit, but I want to acknowledge two incredible women – Ann who quickly became a valued friend and trusted confidant; and Bec, another soul sister, and a friendship forged over exhilarating experiences shared on the other side of the world.

My favourite escape - Elysia Wellness Retreat:

Elysia holds a special place in my heart for many reasons but meeting their Spiritual Healer that set me on the path of 'next level' healing is what I am truly thankful for.

My favourite caffeine and food fix - Two Sisters, Sydney:

My favourite cafe is capably run by the ever-smiling sisters Tayla and Deana. Thank you for indulging my requirement for excellent coffee and food whilst writing this book!

Finally, to my publisher, Pepper Press:

Thank you for taking a chance on me, putting time and effort into shaping the manuscript, and for publishing this book when it seemed no-one else would.

References

Discovering Spirituality
www.hayhouse.com

'Darling Girl'
www.louisehay.com

The Angelic Realms
www.kylegray.co.uk

Divination – Oracle Cards
www.colettebaronreid.com
www.doreenvirtue.com

Elevating and Emerging
www.elysiaretreat.com.au

Soul Retrieval
www.flashpack.com
www.myss.com

The World of Energy Healing Kinesiology
www.consciousenergymedicine.com

Transference Healing
www.transferencehealing.com
www.chironspectra.com
www.astrobutterfly.com

Soul Energy
www.mattkahn.org
www.consciouscoolchic.com
www.mollymccord.online
www.Christopherjpower.com

It happens like this

One day you meet someone and for some inexplicable reason, you feel more connected to this stranger than anyone else—closer to them than your closest family. Perhaps this person carries within them an angel—one sent to you for some higher purpose: to teach you an important lesson or to keep you safe during a perilous time.

What you must do is trust in them—even if they come hand in hand with pain or suffering. The reason for their presence will become clear in due time. Though here is a word of warning: you may grow to love this person but remember they are not yours to keep.

Their purpose isn't to save you but to show you how to save yourself. And once this is fulfilled, the halo lifts and the angel leaves their body as the person exits your life. They will be a stranger to you once more.

Lang Leav,
LOVE & MISADVENTURE

About the Author

Amanda Trenfield owns a successful private consulting practice in Australia which merges her two passions: helping women reinvent and transform their lives, and working with businesses to understand the unique talents of their employees.

www.amandatrenfield.com

Coming Soon from Pepper Press